THE PEOPLE'S DOONESBURY

G.B. TRUDEAU

THE PEOPLE'S
DOONESBURY

NOTES FROM UNDERFOOT, 1978-1980

AN OWL BOOK · HENRY HOLT AND COMPANY · NEW YORK

Copyright © 1978, 1979, 1980, 1981 by G.B. Trudeau
All rights reserved, including the right to reproduce
this book or portions thereof in any form.
Published by Henry Holt and Company, Inc.,
115 West 18th Street, New York, New York 10011.
Published in Canada by Fitzhenry & Whiteside Limited,
195 Allstate Parkway, Markham, Ontario L3R 4T8.

Library of Congress Catalog Card Number: 81-80815
ISBN 0-03-049166-5
ISBN 0-8050-1074-2 (An Owl Book: pbk.)

Henry Holt books are available at special discounts
for bulk purchases for sales promotions, premiums,
fund-raising, or educational use. Special editions
or book excerpts can also be created to specification.

For details contact:

Special Sales Director
Henry Holt and Company, Inc.
115 West 18th Street
New York, New York 10011

Designer: Amy Hill
Printed in the United States of America.

The cartoons in this book have appeared in newspapers
in the United States and abroad under the auspices of
Universal Press Syndicate.

5   7   9   10   8   6   4

*T*o the memory of my friend
and editor, Jim Andrews

AN ANNOTATED CONVERSATION WITH THE AUTHOR

Publisher's Note: For the past several years, the editors of this imprint have sought to persuade cartoonist G. B. Trudeau to go on the record with some thoughts about his life and work. For a few exhilarating weeks before this volume went to press, Trudeau was believed to have been interested. His interest, however, did not blossom into actual consent, so the following interview was regrettably obtained under the false understanding it would only be published in a French film magazine.

As rich in detail as the final transcript was, certain of the artist's references cried out for clarification or addenda, and, for this reason, his remarks have been periodically annotated.

Q: Given all the opportunities you've had, why have you resisted fame these many years?

A: I'm not altogether sure. Perhaps because it requires getting out more than I'd like. If you're serious about it, nurturing a public image, unlike building a reputation, is not something you can do in the privacy of your own living room. It's not just that fame is corrupting; it's time-consuming.[1] You're always busy trying to live up to your latest version of yourself.

Q: Aren't we all?

A: Yes, but it's nice not to have to shave beforehand. Listen, some years ago I did a talk show in Boston. I was twenty-two and I'd been doing the strip for about six months. After a brief introduction, the hostess turned to me and asked what it was like to be rich, famous, and eligible. I hadn't the faintest idea what she was talking about. After staring at her in dumb panic for about five seconds, I finally just rolled my eyes. The hostess looked very pleased and cut to a commercial. I never did another television show.[2]

Q: You must have been tempted, though. I read somewhere that you and Pope John Paul are the only two people ever to have turned down an interview with "60 Minutes."

A: Well, I don't think too much should be made of that. With the Pope, there was a scheduling conflict. They tried to book him on Easter, which is pretty arrogant if you think about it. In my case, I missed the message on my answering service.[3] Unless you've been defrauding widows out of their life savings, "60 Minutes" doesn't call twice.

[1] For Trudeau, so is anonymity. He once hid in his bathroom for three hours to avoid a reporter from the *Baltimore Sun*.

[2] Not entirely true. He did appear on "To Tell the Truth," where only one of the four panelists chose him over the two impostors. Trudeau walked away with $167 and a pair of jade cufflinks.

[3] Trudeau's answering service, VIP of New Haven, played a continuing role in the cartoonist's isolation from the outside world—at least it did until a crate of original strips belonging to Trudeau was removed from its office only to be recovered in a police raid on the Sunshine Girls Escort Service in Hamden, Connecticut. Sunshine's unlucky social director was subsequently convicted of first-degree larceny, partly on the strength of Trudeau's ability to recognize his own work in court.

Q: That sounds a shade ingenuous, but let's go on. . . . You are reported to go to some lengths when you are preparing a sequence in the strip. How much research do you really do?

A: As little as I can possibly get away with. It is for this quality above all others, I think, that I am so admired by undergraduates; I know just enough to create the impression I know a lot. And, of course, being a cartoonist helps. If it weren't for the hopelessly low expectations with which people turn to my section of the newspaper, I'm sure I would have been exposed years ago.

Q: You know, if you're going to continue being self-effacing, we might as well forget the whole thing. Frankly, it's not very interesting. Don't you feel good about yourself?

A: Of course I feel good about myself. You don't think I've got reason to? What's the Pulitzer Prize, chopped liver?[4]

Q: Okay, okay. Tell us about the prize.

A: What's to tell. . . . It's the classiest award in America. No dinner, no acceptance speeches, no TV show. They just call you up and say, "Good going, the check is in the mail." Everybody in my neighborhood was very proud of me. My grocer asked me what I was going to do with the two hundred thousand dollars. I think he thought I won the Pulitzer on a quiz show.[5]

Q: Speaking of easy money, why haven't you gotten into product licensing? The annual gross of the *Peanuts* empire is said to exceed the GNP of your average emerging nation.

A: Well, Sparky Schulz simply takes the position that the spin-offs make people happy. I have no problem with that position, but with the exception of the books, I prefer to keep my characters on the reservation. Perhaps it's because there's no logical connection between my characters and a lunch box. . . unless, of course, you find the logic of the profit motive irresistible.

Q: May we assume you'd loan your characters out for charity?[6]

A: You're missing the point. It's a matter of artistic pride. I think the case against merchandising was best made by the nine-year-old boy who once wrote to inquire why I wasn't selling any *Doonesbury* "by-products."

Q: You seem to be preoccupied with the idea of purity in your work.

[4]When Trudeau, in 1975, became the first comic-strip artist to win the Pulitzer Prize for Editorial Cartooning, the Editorial Cartoonists' Society proposed a resolution condemning the Pulitzer committee. Trudeau, once assured the award was irrevocable, supported the resolution.

[5]The award was actually in the amount of $2,000. Trudeau blew most of it on household bills and some unnecessary minor surgery.

[6]The interviewer's facetiousness was unwarranted. Trudeau had in fact once used several of his characters to promote a Connecticut Red Cross blood drive.

A: Somebody has to be. If you have a good editor, as I had for ten years in Jim Andrews, you come to realize that the inner life of a comic strip is a very fragile ecosystem.[7] It has its own rules, its own time frames, its own internal logic. That logic may be completely askew, but if you tinker with it, the chances are pretty good the whole thing will collapse.

Q: Could you elaborate?

A: Yes, but I'd rather not. I only put in that last bit for people who might be working on dissertations.

Q: That's very thoughtful, but...

A: Look, E. B. White once compared the analysis of humor to dissecting a frog; that is, it can be done, but the frog tends to die in the process.

Q: Where do you see satire going in the decade ahead?

A: You're asking me to predict a trend? You must be mad. I only do postmortems.

Q: All right, where has satire been? What about "Saturday Night Live"?

A: A magnificent missed opportunity. The reason why "SNL" ultimately doesn't matter is that the show never developed a point of view. Originally, the program produced some pretty good guerrilla theater, but with its success, it quickly evolved into a smug exercise in slash-and-burn humor—anarchy for its own sake. Nothing of value was ever left standing. This was a major failing, I think, because great satire has always had some sort of moral underpinnings—just ask Richard Pryor or Lily Tomlin.

Q: Or Garry Trudeau?

A: Yes, but don't look for conviction. I'm like Don Corleone. I've got a business to run.

Q: That's how you justify cuffing people for a living?

A: Absolutely. It's my job. I'm a form of social control. I make no apologies.

Q: Perhaps you should. One of the things that troubles some people about *Doonesbury* is that it's hard to know when you're reporting and when you're making things up. For instance, did Jerry Brown really solicit a political contribution from Sidney Korshak, the alleged organized-crime figure, as you charged in one series?

[7]Andrews realized Trudeau's limitations. He once described the cartoonist as "a thoughtful, creative, and highly concerned young man who is out to make a fast buck."

[8]When asked by NBC reporter Brian Ross, who originally broke the story, why he had solicited a contribution from a man chronically under federal investigation, Brown replied, "Even Jane Fonda was once investigated by the FBI." Later, he described other charges made in the strip as "false and libelous," but declined to press the issue on the novel grounds that "the First Amendment allows libel by the press."

[9]Tom Hayden, among other disinterested observers, wrote that Trudeau's view of Brown was "bigoted."

A: Yes. Actually, Brown doesn't deny this.[8] But most California papers killed the strips on the grounds that I had trampled the rights of a man the FBI had called one of the most influential mobsters in the country. Whimsically enough, the only two papers outside of Brown's home state to share this concern were located in—you guessed it—Reno and Las Vegas.

Q: Do you know Brown personally?

A: Nope. I once met Linda, which, of course, I recognize as not being the same thing.

Q: Some of Brown's admirers charge you've been uncommonly tough on him.[9] Perhaps if you got to know him, you'd feel differently about him.

A: Exactly. Which is as good an excuse as any to pass. One of the reasons why public figures get to be public figures in the first place is that they are not without charm. Insisting, as a George Will does, that one must get in close to make those lovely, nuanced judgment calls is utter nonsense. I'm not interested in private assurances or endearments, the insider's "access." I'm interested in what the outsider sees—the public face the politician *chooses* to project, *chooses* to be judged on. Nothing could be fairer. He's setting the agenda; I'm merely reacting.

Q: You're all heart.

A: Actually, I'm all boy. If you think this business is fun, you're right....

THE ROTUNDA STRIKES BACK

Q: Is it true that Tip O'Neill tried to head off a couple of strips about him during the Korean scandal?

A: Yes, but I think he was getting bad advice. A comic strip is not one of those things you want to look too worried about. One of the strips concerned a dubious nursing-home deal the speaker had drifted into.[1] To the delight of all the papers who picked up the story, this time I actually had my facts straight.[2] The other strip was a mail-in coupon, in which it was implied that Tip was among those who had benefited from Tongsun Park's largesse. It was a shameless gimmick, of course. And since the coupon was then reprinted in all the news stories, readers were given two opportunities to cut it out and send it in.

Q: How many did O'Neill receive?

A: Nobody knows. After the tenth bag of postcards was carted over to the Speaker's office, the post office was alerted to stop delivery. Now *that's* lobbying. It was a gun nut's wet dream.

[1]Gary Hymel, the Speaker's press secretary, offered to show Trudeau cancelled checks that he claimed absolved O'Neill from any impropriety. The offer was quickly withdrawn when Trudeau suggested that their authenticity be verified by *The New York Times.*

[2]And the courage to stand behind them. The artist's long-time mentor and confidant, Nicholas von Hoffman, later commended Trudeau for having the right stuff, saying that he had upheld the highest traditions of "investigative cartooning."

..AND ART BUCHWALD'S NOT AVAILABLE EITHER, WHICH MEANS WE'VE GOT ONLY **ONE** WEEK LEFT TO FIND SOMEONE TO GIVE THIS YEAR'S JOURNALISM LECTURE!

ABE, I'VE GOT A SUGGESTION! HOW ABOUT FORMER AMBASSADOR DUKE, THE EX-GONZO STRINGER FOR "ROLLING STONE"?

HIS IS A UNIQUE PERSPECTIVE ON THE DARK UNDERSIDE OF OUTLAW JOURNALISM. AND HIS IMMENSE POPULARITY AMONG US KIDS WOULD LEND A CACHET TO THE LECTURE!

ACCORDING TO WHOM?

ZONKER. I'VE NEVER HEARD OF HIM MYSELF.

TRUST ME, GUYS. HE'D BE PERFECT! REALLY!

GOOD LORD, KID, IT'S ONLY SEVEN O'CLOCK! HAVEN'T YOU EVER HEARD OF TIME ZONES?

YES, SIR, I'M SORRY, SIR, BUT WE'RE KIND OF PRESSED. YOUR NEPHEW SAID IT WOULD BE OKAY TO CALL..

MY NEPHEW? ZONKER?

YES, SIR. HE'S ON THE SPEAKER'S COMMITTEE WITH ME..

LOOK, CHIEF, I DON'T GIVE A DAMN IF HE'S ON THE SAME..

AND HE SAID TO BE SURE TO MENTION THE $3,000. HONORARIUM TO YOU!

THAT RASCAL. HE REALLY SAID THAT?

YES, SIR. HE SEEMS TO THINK THE WORLD OF YOU.

E 8

MR. DUKE! MR. **DUKE!** OVER HERE, SIR!

E 8

HELLO?

I'M RONNIE, SIR! DID YOU HAVE A GOOD FLIGHT?

YEAH, IT WAS OKAY.

LET ME JUST SAY, SIR, HOW VERY HONORED WE ALL ARE THAT YOU WERE ABLE TO TAKE TIME FROM YOUR BUSY SCHEDULE TO COME SPEAK TO US!

UH-HUH. GOT MY FEE WITH YOU?

OH, YES, OF COURSE, SIR. IN TENS AND TWENTIES, AS REQUESTED.

WELL, SIR, I'LL BE BY IN A FEW HOURS TO TAKE YOU TO YOUR LECTURE. IF YOU NEED ANYTHING, JUST..

WELL, KID, AS A MATTER OF FACT, I WILL BE NEEDING A FEW THINGS.

UM.. EVERYTHING ON THIS LIST, SIR?

YES. IT'S VERY IMPORTANT. I'M GOING TO BE DOING A LITTLE WRITING TONIGHT, AND I'LL NEED SUPPLIES!

"ONE IBM SELECTRIC TYPEWRITER, ONE CRATE OF FRESH GRAPEFRUIT, THREE CASES OF WILD TURKEY.."

IF I HAVE TO GO OUT FOR ALL THAT MYSELF, IT'LL BREAK MY CONCENTRATION!

"TWO ALBINO TYPISTS, ONE TRAMPOLINE.."

SAY, YOU DON'T KNOW IF THESE ROOMS HAVE SPRINKLERS, DO YOU?

PROFESSOR KISSINGER, OL' WEINBURGER HERE'S BEEN MAKING A PRETTY STRONG CASE AGAINST GOING TO THE SHA-NA-NA'S DINNER! WHAT'S YOUR REPLY?

HEY, BARNEY..

NO, NO, IT'S ONLY FAIR! LET HIM GIVE HIS SIDE!

THANK YOU, MR. PERKINS. I'M GRATEFUL TO FINALLY HAVE A CHANCE TO PUT THE DINNER AND ITS SPONSOR IN THE PROP- ER PERSPECTIVE..

SPONSOR?

THE FRIENDS OF EXXON SOCIETY WAS FOUNDED IN..

NEVER MIND.

GOOD EVENING. THIS IS THE SCENE IN NEW YORK TONIGHT AS HUNDREDS OF DEMONSTRATORS GATHER OUT- SIDE A DINNER FOR THE EMPRESS OF IRAN. ROLAND HEDLEY IS THERE.

HARRY, THERE'S BEEN A SLIGHT DELAY IN THE FESTIVITIES TONIGHT AS WE AWAIT THE LATE ARRIVAL OF PRO-SHAH FORCES HERE AT THE NEW YORK HILTON HOTEL.

BAD WEATHER APPARENTLY DELAYED THE BUSES BRINGING THE SHAH'S RE- CRUITS TO N.Y., SO OUT OF FAIRNESS, PLANNERS HAVE HELD UP THE BANQUET TO ALLOW COUNTERDEMONSTRATORS TIME TO TAKE UP THEIR POSITIONS!

LONG LIVE THE SHAH!

..AND HERE THEY COME NOW!! LOOKS LIKE THE EVENING'S UNDER WAY, HARRY!

HARRY, I'M TALKING TO A COUPLE OF STUDENTS RIGHT NOW, BUT UN- LIKE MOST OF THE FOREIGN DEMON- STRATORS HERE, THESE YOUNG MEN ARE AS AMERICAN AS YOU OR I!

MOREOVER, I AM TOLD THAT THEY ARE STUDENTS OF DR. HENRY KISSINGER, THE FEATURED SPEAK- ER AT TONIGHT'S DINNER HON- ORING THE EMPRESS!

GENTLEMEN, TELL ME, WHY ON EARTH ARE YOU WEARING THOSE MASKS? SURELY YOU'RE NOT PROTECTING RELATIVES OR LOVED ONES IN IRAN?

NO, BUT WE'VE GOT MIDTERMS COMING UP, MAN..

WHOA! SAY NO MORE!

HEY, LOOK! IT'S SHIRLEY MACLAINE!

SHIRLEY MACLAINE? I DON'T BELIEVE IT! WHAT'S SHE DOING HERE?

HEY, SHIRL! WHAT GIVES? DON'T YOU KNOW WHAT HAPPENS TO POLITICAL DISSIDENTS IN IRAN?

FOR YOUR INFORMATION, FELLAH, IRANIAN DISSIDENTS ARE SENT TO THE SHAH'S PRISONS, WHERE THEY ARE INTERROGATED, BRUTALIZED, AND RARELY HEARD FROM AGAIN!

OH. YOU HEARD, THEN.

THAT'S RIGHT. SO YOU CAN STOP ACTING SO DAMN SUPERIOR!

THIS IS ROLAND HEDLEY. TODAY AMBASSADOR NGUYEN VAN PHRED WAS INSTALLED AS THE NEW VIETNAMESE ENVOY TO THE U.N.! ABC WAS THERE WITH THE TOUGH QUESTIONS..

MR. PHRED, HAVE YOU BEEN TO STUDIO 54 YET?

NO. I WAS NOT SENT HERE TO DANCE.

DO YOU KNOW WHERE YOU'LL BE LIVING YET, SIR?

I JUST GOT HERE.. I HAVEN'T HAD TIME TO LOOK. I HEAR THE WEST SIDE IS NICE..

HOW ABOUT A SUIT? WILL YOU BE GETTING A NEW SUIT?

UM.. NO.. WHY?

THIS IS INDEED AN HONOR, MR. PHRED! WE DIDN'T EXPECT VIETNAM TO SEND A REPLACEMENT SO QUICKLY!

WELL, AS YOU KNOW, MR. YOUNG, MY COUNTRY IS FULL OF SURPRISES. BESIDES, OUR U.N. MISSION HERE IS TOO IMPORTANT FOR IT TO REMAIN VACANT FOR LONG!

OUR FEELINGS EXACTLY, MR. AMBASSADOR! AGAIN, ON BEHALF OF THE UNITED STATES, LET ME OFFER YOU THE WARMEST WELCOME TO OUR COUNTRY!

BUT NO MORE SPYING, OKAY?

ME? NO WAY! "LEAVE IT TO THE PROS" IS MY MOTTO!

EXCUSE ME? COULD YOU HELP ME?

THAT'S WHAT I'M HERE FOR, SIR! THIS IS **YOUR** UNITED NATIONS!

COULD YOU DIRECT ME TO THE SECURITY COUNCIL CHAMBER?

I'M AFRAID IT'S NOT IN SESSION RIGHT NOW, SIR. BUT REST ASSURED, THE STRUGGLE FOR PEACE GOES ON EVERY DAY!

IT DOES?

THAT'S RIGHT! AROUND THE CLOCK!

WHERE 'BOUTS?

FIRST DOOR ON YOUR LEFT. PLOWSHARES LOUNGE.

UM.. EXCUSE ME, SIR, I THINK YOU'RE IN MY SEAT.

WELL, HELLO! YOU MUST BE AMBASSADOR NGUYEN VAN PHRED, FROM VIETNAM!

WHY, YES, THAT'S RIGHT!

WELCOME TO OUR LITTLE WORKSHOP FOR PEACE, PHRED! I'M VICTOR PINTO, AMBASSADOR PLENIPOTENTIARY FROM BENIN!

BENIN? UM.. ARE WE ON GOOD TERMS?

WELL, OF COURSE! WE'RE IN THE SAME VOTING BLOC!

FORGIVE ME. I LEFT MY BRIEFING BOOK ON THE PLANE, SEE..

PEACOCK, I REPEAT: WE'VE LANDED LAGOS, REQUEST MINI-CAMS FOR J.C.'S MOTORCADE POOL!

ALSO, TELL NEW YORK WE'RE BOUNCING EVENING NEWS FEED OFF THE BIRD AT 5:30 EST!

ROGER, WILCO! OUT!

BZZ!..BIP! CALLING STAR QUALITY! THIS IS VERTICAL HOLD! COME IN, STAR QUALITY!

"STAR QUALITY"?

GO AHEAD, VERTICAL HOLD! DO WE HAVE A ROGER FROM HAIR SPRAY?

WELL, SO MUCH FOR LAGOS! DID YOU CATCH MY STAND-UP TODAY, RICK?

NO, I'M AFRAID I MISSED IT, ROLAND. ANOTHER ELECTRIC PERFORMANCE?

WELL, IT WASN'T BAD! CAN'T BEAT THE IMMEDIACY OF TELEVISION, YOU KNOW, RICK?

YEAH! ESPECIALLY WITH A STORY LIKE CARTER'S LATEST OPEN-MIKE BLUNDER!

HIS WHAT?

WE'RE PLAYING IT PAGE ONE! IT HAS TO BE THE BIGGEST GAFFE HE'S EVER MADE, WOULDN'T YOU SAY?

UH..YEAH! WHAT WERE HIS EXACT WORDS AGAIN?

I DUNNO, I JUST HOPE SADAT DOESN'T OVERREACT, YOU KNOW?

..AND THEN THE CAMERA CUTS BACK TO ME ON A MEDIUM CLOSE-UP AS I SAY, "WAS THE CARTER JOURNEY A SUCCESS? ONLY TIME WILL TELL!"

HERE I DROP MY VOICE..."BUT IF THERE WAS ANYTHING OF SUBSTANCE TO BE DIVINED FROM THIS TRIP, IT COMPLETELY ESCAPED THE ATTENTION OF THIS REPORTER!"

THAT'S IT?

YUP. WHAT DO YOU THINK?

SURE YOU CAN AFFORD TO BE THAT HONEST?

HELL, YES! I CALL 'EM AS I SEE 'EM, RICK!

WELL, IT'S BEEN A PLEASURE RIDING WITH YOU, REDFERN! GIVE MY BEST TO EVERYONE AT THE "TIMES"!

TAP! TAP!

NBC News

THE "POST."

OH, RIGHT, THE WASHINGTON "POST." GOOD PAPER, THAT.

TAP! TAP!

NBC News

THANK YOU.

WHAT HAVE YOU PEOPLE BEEN UP TO SINCE YOU OVERTHREW THE GOVERNMENT, ANYWAY?

NBC News

NOT SURE. SPORTS, I THINK.

BET YOU GUYS MISS THE HECK OUT OF THE TRICKSTER, HUH?

TAP! TAP!

NBC News

SO MUCH FOR MR. CARTER'S NOD TO THE THIRD WORLD! DID YOU KNOW HE'S ALREADY HOME?

WELL, OF COURSE, PHRED! HE HAS TO HOST THE ANNUAL HUMAN RIGHTS AWARDS BANQUET THIS WEEK!

OH, SAY, THAT'S RIGHT! YOU SENT IN YOUR NOMINATION FORM YET?

YOU BETTER BELIEVE IT! WITH ALL THIS NEW INTEREST IN AFRICA, BENIN FINALLY HAS A REAL CHANCE!

LOOK AT THE CURVE ON THIS CHART WE PREPARED! THE INCIDENCE OF CURTAILED LIBERTIES HAS DROPPED OFF SIGNIFICANTLY! AND CHECK OUT THESE BEFORE-AND-AFTER PHOTOS OF TYPICAL POLITICAL PRISONERS!

WOW! WHAT A DIFFERENCE!

COMPLETELY UNRETOUCHED! AND WE GOT AFFIDAVITS, TOO!

VICTOR, HOW'D THIS HUMAN RIGHTS AWARDS BANQUET GET STARTED ANYWAY?

WELL, AS I UNDERSTAND IT, IT'S THE BRAINCHILD OF THE U.S. SECRETARY OF SYMBOLISM.

EVERY YEAR, HE PRESENTS AWARDS TO THOSE NATIONS WHO SHOW THE MOST IMPROVEMENT IN FURTHERING PERSONAL LIBERTIES, AS CERTIFIED BY AMNESTY INTERNATIONAL!

HERE, TAKE A LOOK! IT'S ALL EXPLAINED IN THIS WHITE HOUSE BROCHURE OUTLINING THE AWARDS AND THEIR QUALIFICATIONS..

"THE JAMES EARL CARTER ATONEMENT CUP, GIVEN EACH YEAR TO.."

THAT'S THE MOST COVETED, OF COURSE.

WELL, SEE YOU AT THE HUMAN RIGHTS BANQUET, VICTOR!

OKAY, PHRED! I MIGHT BE A LITTLE LATE. I'VE GOT TO DO SOME LAST MINUTE LOBBYING..

THE COMPETITION'S THAT INTENSE, HUH?

ARE YOU KIDDING? BILLIONS IN U.S. AID CAN HANG ON THE OUTCOME! YOU CAN'T BELIEVE THE LENGTHS SOME COUNTRIES GO TO!

WHY, LAST YEAR, PRESIDENT MARCOS OF THE PHILIPPINES EVEN TRIED RESTORING DEMOCRACY A WEEK BEFORE THE DEADLINE! OF COURSE, IT DIDN'T WORK.

NO AWARD?

NO DEMOCRACY. TURNED OUT HIS PEOPLE WEREN'T READY FOR IT.

GOOD EVENING, FRIENDS, AND WELCOME TO THE SECOND ANNUAL HUMAN RIGHTS AWARDS BANQUET!

BEFORE WE GET STARTED, I'D JUST LIKE TO SAY THAT THESE AWARDS WOULDN'T BE POSSIBLE IF NOT FOR REPORTS FURNISHED US BY HUMAN RIGHTS WATCHDOG AMNESTY INTERNATIONAL!

BOOOO!! BOOO! HISSS!

AND WELL YOU MIGHT BOO!

HA! HA, HA! HA, HA! HA! HA!

BOY, THERE SURE ARE A LOT OF CATEGORIES..

YES, THEY'VE EXPANDED IT CONSIDERABLY FROM LAST YEAR.

IT'S A SHAME, REALLY. I THINK THEY'VE DEVALUED THE HUMAN RIGHTS AWARDS BY OFFERING SO MANY..

LADIES AND GENTLEMEN, MAY I HAVE YOUR ATTENTION, PLEASE? IN OUR FIRST CATEGORY..

HERE WE GO! NEED A PENCIL?

FOR MOST COURTEOUS CUSTOMS OFFICIALS..

TEN BUCKS ON BERMUDA!

HMM.. THEY STILL USING PINK JEEPS?

FOR MOST IMPROVED HUMAN RIGHTS CLIMATE IN A DEVELOPING NATION..

WE'VE GOT IT! I JUST KNOW WE'VE GOT IT!

BENIN'S A CHANGED COUNTRY, PHRED! CIVIL LIBERTIES AND THEN SOME! LAST YEAR ALONE WE RELEASED OVER 50 POLITICAL PRISONERS!

..AND THE WINNER IS.. GUINEA!

WHAT?!

GEE, VICTOR, I'M REALLY SORRY..

THAT DOES IT! BACK IN THE SLAMMER!

..AND THE WINNER OF MOST IMPROVED CLIMATE FOR PUBLIC DEBATE WITHIN AN AUTHORITARIAN POLITICAL REGIME IS.. NICARAGUA!

YEAAA! BRAVO! BRAVO! CLAP! CLAP!

CLAP! CLAP!

CLAP!

CLAP! CLAP!

THANK YOU VERY MUCH! I'D JUST LIKE TO SAY THAT THE REFORMS IN MY COUNTRY WERE A DIRECT RESULT OF PRESSURE FROM THE U.S.!

UNITED STATES PRESSURE! ISN'T THAT GREAT, LADIES AND GENTLEMEN?!

IF YOU GUYS HADN'T PUT THE SCREWS ON, WE'D STILL BE IN THE DARK AGES!

CLAP CLAP

..AND THE FINAL AWARD OF THE EVENING GOES TO THAT NATION WHOSE SENSE OF MISSION AND HIGH MORAL PURPOSE MOST CLOSELY RESEMBLES THAT OF THE UNITED STATES!

>RIP!< .. AND THE WINNER IS..

WHOA.. WHAT HAVE WE GOT HERE? IT LOOKS LIKE A NINE-WAY TIE!

IT'S.. WESTERN EUROPE!

ACCEPTING FOR THE WEST IS NATO'S ALEXANDER HAIG..

GOOD MORNING! I'M MARK SLACK-MEYER, AND THIS IS "PROFILES ON PARADE"!

TODAY WE'RE PLEASED TO HAVE BACK WITH US DR. DAN ASHER, AUTHOR OF THE PHENOMENALLY SUCCESSFUL "MELLOW: HOW TO GET IT"! WELCOME BACK, DAN!

UH..DAN?

OH, SORRY, MARK. I WAS FLASHING ON MY MANTRA.

I'M TALKING TO MELLOW EXPERT DR. DAN ASHER. DAN, TELL US, WHAT EXACTLY IS MELLOW?

GOOD QUESTION, MARK. I CAN REALLY RELATE TO IT..

BASICALLY, MELLOW IS A NEW WAY OF DEFINING THE SPACE YOUR HEAD'S IN, A WAY OF GETTING IN TOUCH WITH THOSE FEELINGS THAT WILL ENABLE YOU TO LEAD A MUCH MORE NATURAL LIFE-STYLE.

I SEE. AND WHAT WOULD BE SOME EXAMPLES OF MELLOW?

MELLOW IS ALL AROUND US, MARK. IT'S WHEAT FIBER. IT'S HOUSEPLANTS. IT'S CHOPIN FESTIVALS AND JACUZZIS AND TENNIS LESSONS AND THE ACLU!

HMM..SOUNDS COMPLICATED. IS THERE BEGINNER'S MELLOW?

OH, FOR SURE! ALL YOU NEED IS A GOOD TEN-SPEED!

DAN, I THINK THE QUESTION THAT MANY PEOPLE MIGHT HAVE FOR YOU NOW IS, "WHAT WITH ALL THE CUISINARTS, TENNIS LESSONS AND TR-4'S, CAN I REALLY AFFORD MELLOW?"

I HEAR YOU, MARK. ONE OF THE MOST COMMON MISCONCEPTIONS ABOUT MELLOW TODAY IS THAT YOU HAVE TO BE UPWARDLY MOBILE, ECONOMICWISE, BEFORE YOU CAN FLASH ON IT!

WELL, IT JUST ISN'T SO! IN FACT, THE EXTENSIVE RESEARCH I DID DURING MY FELLOWSHIP AT THE CALIFORNIA INSTITUTE FOR THE MELLOW STRONGLY SUGGESTS OTHERWISE!

FELLOWSHIP? YOU WERE A MELLOW FELLOW?

IT'S ALL IN MY CHAPTER, "MELLOW ON A FIXED INCOME."

I'M STILL TALKING TO DR. DAN ASHER, AUTHOR OF THE BEST-SELLING "MELLOW: HOW TO GET IT," AND A FELLOW AT THE CALIFORNIA INSTITUTE FOR THE MELLOW..

DAN, I WONDER IF WE SHOULDN'T OPEN UP THE LINES NOW, AND GIVE OUR LISTENERS A CHANCE TO RAP WITH YOU.

HEY, FOR SURE, MARK!

OKAY, FOLKS, IF YOU'VE GOT ANY QUESTIONS FOR MELLOW EXPERT DAN ASHER, FROM HOW TO GET IN TOUCH WITH YOUR FEELINGS TO HOW TO JOIN THE SIERRA CLUB, WHY DON'T YOU GIVE US A RING!

RRING!

MELLOW HOTLINE! WHERE'S YOUR HEAD AT?

HEY, WILL YOU GUYS JUST SHUT UP AND PLAY A KISS RECORD?

THIS IS MELLOW HOTLINE! WHERE'S YOUR HEAD AT?

IT'S IN A BAD PLACE, DAN. I'M INCREDIBLY BUMMED OUT!

WHAT WENT DOWN, SEE, IS THAT MY LOVER AND I HAD MY EX OVER FOR DINNER, AND, LIKE, WE GOT INTO THIS INCREDIBLE HIGH-ENERGY RAP ON WHALES Y'KNOW?

WELL, MY LOVER COULDN'T HANDLE THE TRIP, AND EVER SINCE, HE'S BEEN DOING A REAL ANXIETY NUMBER ON ME, AND LIKE, WE HAVEN'T BEEN ABLE TO RELATE TO EACH OTHER FOR WEEKS!

HMM..HAVE YOU TRIED JOGGING TOGETHER?

YEAH, BUT YOU KNOW SCORPIOS. COMMITMENT-WISE, THERE'S NO PERCENTAGE IN IT!

HELLO, THIS IS MELLOW HOTLINE! WHERE'S YOUR HEAD AT?

UM..YEAH, I'D JUST LIKE TO SAY, LIKE..UM, Y'KNOW, LIKE, Y'KNOW, I'M, LIKE, Y'KNOW, UM..Y'KNOW?

FOR SURE, MAN. I KNOW JUST WHERE YOU'RE COMING FROM.

YOU DO?

FOR SURE! YOU'RE HAVING A HEAD TRIP. YOU'RE IN THIS WEIRD SPACE.

OH, WOW.. YEAH, I CAN RELATE TO THAT! THANKS A LOT, DAN!

YOU SURE GIVE GOOD MELLOW, DAN.

HEY, I WROTE THE BOOK, DIDN'T I?

DUKE, THERE'S NO WAY WE'RE GONNA GET ANY OF THESE KIDS! THE BEST OF THEM WILL BE ALL GONE BY ROUND SEVEN.

SEVEN? WE CAN'T MAKE A PICK UNTIL ROUND SEVEN?

THAT'S RIGHT. OUR TOP DRAFT CHOICES HAVE BEEN LONG SINCE TRADED AWAY..

A POX ON GEORGE ALLEN! NO WONDER THE TALENTLESS TOAD BOLTED TOWN WHEN HE DID!

TELL ME ABOUT IT. THIS IS THE THIRD YEAR I'VE HAD TO JUNK MY SCOUTING REPORTS!

I JUST DON'T SEE HOW HE GOT AWAY WITH THAT "THE FUTURE IS NOW" GARBAGE AS LONG AS HE DID!

I GUESS BECAUSE NOBODY ELSE HERE UNDERSTOOD POETRY.

YEAH, WELL, THINGS ARE GOING TO CHANGE AROUND HERE!

WELL, DUKE, IF WE CAN'T DRAFT, WE MIGHT AS WELL GO SHOPPING. GOT ANY FREE AGENTS YOU LIKE?

YEAH, HOW ABOUT "LAVA-LAVA" LENNY? YOU FAMILIAR WITH "LAVA-LAVA'S" WORK?

NOPE. WHO IS HE?

A KID I DISCOVERED SLINGING COCONUTS DURING MY TENURE IN PAGO PAGO. HE'S NOW PLAYING FRONT FOUR FOR THE LIONS.

ALL FRONT FOUR?

BIG? BOBBY, THE OPPOSITION'S LUCKY IF IT EVEN GETS A GLIMPSE OF THE QUARTERBACK!

SOUNDS LIKE A BIG BOY..

UH-HUH..

I'M NOT KIDDING! WHEN I FIRST SAW HIM IN SAMOA, I THOUGHT HE WAS AN OFFSHORE ISLAND!

SO TELL ME MORE ABOUT THIS "LAVA-LAVA" LENNY, DUKE..

WELL, TO BEGIN WITH, HE'S THE BIGGEST LINEMAN TO COME OUT OF THE PACIFIC IN TWENTY YEARS!

THEY'RE SO RESPECTFUL OF HIS TALENTS IN DETROIT THAT HE HAS HIS OWN HANDLER! THIS KID HAS TO BE SEEN TO BE BELIEVED!

ANY PERSONALITY QUIRKS?

NONE THAT I'M AWARE OF. UNLESS YOU WANT TO INCLUDE A VILE TEMPER.

OH? WHAT'S HE PLAY ON?

FRESH PINEAPPLE. THEY FEED HIM AFTER EVERY TACKLE.

WHAT IS IT, BEV?

MR. DUKE, "LAVA-LAVA" LENNY'S ATTORNEY IS ON THE LINE.

THANKS, BABE. PUT HIM ON.. HELLO, HOOK? IT'S DUKE!

HI, THERE, DUKE! YOU GET MY CONTRACT PROPOSAL YET?

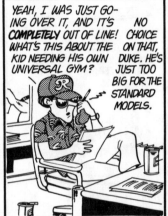

YEAH, I WAS JUST GOING OVER IT, AND IT'S COMPLETELY OUT OF LINE! WHAT'S THIS ABOUT THE KID NEEDING HIS OWN UNIVERSAL GYM?

NO CHOICE ON THAT, DUKE. HE'S JUST TOO BIG FOR THE STANDARD MODELS.

OH, YEAH? WELL, HOW ABOUT HIS OWN MEAT LOCKER?

HE'S A GROWING BOY, DUKE! LOOK, YOU WANT A COMPETITOR OR NOT?

OKAY, HOOK, YOU'RE ROBBING ME BLIND, BUT I THINK WE CAN WORK SOMETHING OUT..

I'M GLAD TO HEAR IT, DUKE.

FRANKLY, THE 'SKINS NEED "LAVA-LAVA", AND I'LL BE WILLING TO MAKE YOU A FIRM OFFER ON MONDAY!

MONDAY? WHY NOT NOW?

I GOTTA CONFER WITH THE MONEY, HOOK. YOU UNDERSTAND. JUST A FORMALITY.

OKAY, MONDAY IT IS. I'LL PREPARE MY CLIENT.

THANKS, HOOK. YOU'RE A PRINCE.

I KNOW. HOW DO YOU WANT HIM SHIPPED?

THAT'S RIGHT, MIKE, IN THE EIGHTH AND NINTH ROUNDS, DRAFT THEM BOTH! WE'RE STILL WEAK IN THE MIDDLE!

THE HELL WE ARE!

HUH?

YOUR PRAYERS HAVE BEEN ANSWERED, BOBBY BOY! GUESS WHO JUST SIGNED WITH YOURS TRULY?

NOT "LAVA-LAVA"?

390 LBS. OF STEAMING SAMOAN! OUR FRONT FOUR PROBLEMS ARE OVER!

MIKE? CANCEL THAT ORDER OF BUCKEYES!

BARTENDER! CHAMPAGNE FOR EVERYONE ON MR. WILLIAMS!

DAD! I DON'T BELIEVE IT! WHAT ARE *YOU* DOING HERE?

I MIGHT ASK YOU THE SAME QUESTION. DON'T YOU HAVE EXAMS THIS WEEK?

UH.. NO. I TOOK THE SEMESTER OFF, TO WORK AT THE RADIO STATION.

THE RADIO STATION.

RIGHT.

I SEE. AND THE FAB FOUR ARE WELL?

NO. THEY SPLIT UP. LOOK, DAD, I WAS GOING TO WRITE ..

NO, NOTHING NEW AT HOME. IT'S BEEN A QUIET SPRING.

AW, C'MON, DAD, THAT'S WHAT YOU ALWAYS SAY. I'M SURE YOU TWO HAVE BEEN UP TO *SOMETHING*..

NO, NOTHING! WHAT DO YOU WANT? WE LIVE IN NORTHERN NEW JERSEY, FOR GOD'S SAKE!

OH, I HAD ANOTHER HEART ATTACK.

SEE? NOW, I BET THERE'S A LOT OF STUFF LIKE THAT.

YOU KNOW, AS MUCH AS I HATE THESE THINGS, I HAVE TO ADMIT I'M LOOKING FORWARD TO SEEING MY OLD ROOM-MATES AGAIN..

OH, YEAH?

BELIEVE IT OR NOT, THE LAST TIME WE WERE ALL TOGETHER WAS AFTER THE REGATTA IN 1943. WE THREW A BEER PARTY BEHIND THE BOATHOUSE WITH SOME GIRLS FROM THE VASSAR GLEE CLUB. WHAT A TIME THAT WAS..

YOU KNOW, IF SHE JUST HADN'T MARRIED STAN, I'LL BET WE..

CAREFUL, DAD. YOU'RE FREE ASSO-CIATING.

ACTUALLY, I'M NOT DOING THAT MUCH AT THE FIRM ANYMORE. THE KIDS HAVE PRETTY MUCH TAKEN OVER..

MY OLDEST, TED, IS SOMETHING OF A COMMODITIES WIZ, AND JENNIFER CALLS OPTIONS BETTER 'N HER OL' MAN! HEE, HEE! CAN YOU IMAGINE?

VERY IMPRESSIVE, ROGER.

SO HOW ABOUT YOU, GUY? GOT ANY KIDS?

NO. NONE TO SPEAK OF.

HUH?

REALLY? NOT EVEN ONE IN LAW SCHOOL?

WHO IS IT, BERNIE?

YOU KNOW A ROLAND BURTON HEDLEY, JR. ZONK?

UH.. NO. NO, I DON'T.

TRENDS, ZONKER! THAT'S WHERE I'M AT THESE DAYS! ROONE'S VERY CONCERNED THAT ABC NEWS HAVE ITS OWN MOOD MAN!

SO THAT'S WHY I WAS HOPING YOU MIGHT BE ABLE TO TURN ME ON TO ANY NEW TRENDS HERE IN YOUR NECK OF THE WOODS..

WELL, I'M NOT SURE I CAN HELP YOU THERE, ROLLIE..

TO TELL YOU THE TRUTH, THE PROBLEM IS ONE OF OVERKILL. THERE'RE SO MANY TRENDS SWEEPING THE NATION THESE DAYS, IT'S HARD TO FIND ONE TO REALLY CALL YOUR OWN!

TAKE YOUR MAGAZINES, FOR INSTANCE. DURING THE SAME WEEK RECENTLY, "TIME" AND "NEWSWEEK" RAN COVER STORIES ON THE COOKING CRAZE AND THE DIETING CRAZE..

IN OTHER WORDS, ACCORDING TO OUR MAJOR NEWSWEEKLIES, THE TWO HOTTEST TRENDS IN THE COUNTRY ARE EATING AND NOT EATING!

SO WHO KNOWS? LATELY I'VE BEEN THINKING OF JUST STRIKING OUT ON MY OWN..

GOOD PLAN. I HEAR MORE AND MORE PEO- PLE ARE DOING THAT THESE DAYS.

GBTrudeau

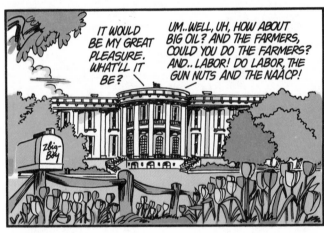

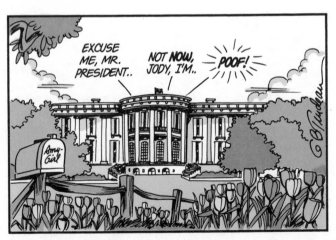

HI, THIS IS ABC! FREDDY SILVERMAN'S OFFICE!

HELLO, THIS IS IRWIN NUMBERS AT NBC. IS FRED IN?

I'M SORRY, SIR, MR. SILVERMAN'S ABC CONTRACT IS NOT UP UNTIL NEXT WEEK. HE IS NOT PERMITTED TO..

TO TALK TO ME, YES, I KNOW. COULD YOU GIVE HIM A MESSAGE FOR ME, THEN? IT'S VERY IMPORTANT!

VERY WELL, SIR.

TELL HIM WE'RE ON THE VERGE OF ANNOUNCING THE NEW SHOW WE DISCUSSED, BUT THAT THERE'S REAL CONCERN THAT THE STAR ISN'T STACKED ENOUGH.

I'LL SEE THAT HE GETS THE MESSAGE, SIR.

TELL HIM IT'S URGENT, OKAY? WE'VE ALREADY GOT TWO SHOWS IN THE CAN.

WE'RE REALLY APPRECIATIVE YOU COULD COME OVER FOR A PEEK AT THE SHOW, FRED..

FREDDY!

THE NAME IS FREDDY! NEVER CALL ME FRED! WHEN'RE YOU PEOPLE GOING TO LEARN? TO PROGRAM FOR NINE-YEAR-OLDS, YOU HAVE TO THINK LIKE ONE!

IF YOU WANT NBC TO START CLICKING AGAIN, YOU'RE GOING TO HAVE TO STOP ACTING LIKE GROWN MEN! UNDERSTOOD?

YES, FREDDY.

GOOD. NOW, LET'S TAKE A LOOK AT YOUR CLEAVAGE SITUATION.

RIGHT. OKAY, IN THIS FIRST EPISODE, THE PLOT CALLED FOR WET T-SHIRTS..

LET ME SET IT UP FOR YOU, FREDDY. THE GUY ON THE LEFT IS LEONARD. HE RUNS A WOMEN'S HEALTH SPA IN LOS ANGELES!

OUR JIGGLE INTEREST IS MUFFY, THE PHYSICAL THERAPIST. THE RUNNING GAG IS THAT EVERY TIME LEONARD GOES IN TO CHECK THE SAUNA, THERE'S MUFFY!

WE THINK THAT CHRISSY LANG, THE GIRL WHO PLAYS MUFFY, IS A MAJOR, BUT MAJOR, TALENT! WE THINK SHE COULD MAKE "SPA" THE HOTTEST SHOW ON T.V.!

GREAT STUFF. DOES SHE HAVE ANY LINES?

WELL, NOT AT FIRST. WE WANT TO ESTABLISH HER CHARACTER.

..AND THE VIEWER SOON SEES THAT LEONARD'S FAMILY IS A LOT LIKE HIS OWN, ONLY MUCH ZANIER!

DON'T TALK WITH YOUR MOUTH FULL, DEAR!

AW, MOM!

NOW, THIS NEXT BIT INTRODUCES SALLY, THE TEEN-AGED DAUGHTER.

HEY! LOOK WHO'S FINALLY UP!

'MORNING, EVERYONE!

HEY! FULL FRONTAL NUDITY! I LOVE IT!

WELL, WAIT'LL YOU SEE THE PREDICAMENTS SHE GETS IN!

ANYONE SEEN MY SHAMPOO?

THIS IS ROLAND BURTON HEDLEY, JR.! AT ROCKEFELLER CENTER TONIGHT, TENSIONS ARE MOUNTING AS THE NBC TELEVISION NETWORK AWAITS ITS NEW MESSIAH, FRED P. SILVERMAN.

CAN THE GENIUS BEHIND "THE LOVE BOAT" AND "CAPTAIN CAVEMAN AND THE TEENANGELS" RESTORE THE FORTUNES OF LAST-PLACE NBC? A RECENT DEVELOPMENT SUGGESTS HE MIGHT..

ABC WIDE WORLD OF NEWS HAS LEARNED THAT WHEN FREDDY SILVERMAN ARRIVES AT NBC THIS WEEK, HE WILL PROPOSE A POLICY OF PRIME-TIME FRONTAL NUDITY!

ALSO, CHIMPS. BUT WE'LL GET TO THAT LATER. FOR DETAILS ON THE NUDITY, LET'S GO TO CHICAGO..

CHICAGO?

YES, AS THE COUNTDOWN CONTINUES, THE NAME OF THE GAME AT NBC IS "WAITING FOR FREDDY."

CAN SILVERMAN TURN THINGS AROUND FOR THE LOWLY NETWORK? WELL, IT'S ANYONE'S GUESS. IN THE RATINGS GAME THERE IS ONLY ONE QUESTION: HOW LOW ARE YOU WILLING TO SINK?

NO ONE, IT SEEMS, IS IMMUNE. EVEN THE NEW TAG-TEAM ANCHOR FORMAT RIGHT HERE AT ABC WIDE WORLD OF NEWS WAS ADOPTED AS A DESPERATE, LAST-DITCH RESPONSE TO SAGGING RATINGS.

BACK TO YOU, FRANK, PETER, AND MAX.   THANKS.

THANK YOU, ROLLIE.

YES, THANKS. IN OTHER NEWS..

THE LONG VIGIL IS OVER. EVEN AS I SPEAK, FRED P. SILVERMAN IS SPINNING HIS MILLION-DOLLAR WHEELS FOR THIRD-PLACE NBC!

ALREADY, THE NEW MAN HAS BEGUN TO LIVE UP TO HIS IMAGE AS A HARD WORKER. SILVERMAN IS SAID TO HAVE REPORTED TO WORK THIS MORNING AT 5:30 A.M.!

AND NOW, AMIDST GROWING RUMORS THAT THEIR NEW BOSS EVEN SKIPPED LUNCH, NBC EXECUTIVES ARE ANXIOUSLY AWAITING THE OUTCOME OF FREDDY'S PROGRAMING MAGIC!

ANY CHANGE YET?

YES..YES! BY GOD, HE'S TURNING IT AROUND!

LOOK OUT, WONDER CHIMP!

BLAM! BLAM!

FRED SILVERMAN. ON TOP. THE MAN OF THE MOMENT. BUT WHAT OF THE LOSERS? WHAT HAPPENS TO THEM? CORRESPONDENT ROLAND HEDLEY TALKED TO THE SECRETARY OF NBC'S DEPOSED HERB SCHLOSSER.

MISS JENKINS, WHAT WAS IT LIKE TO WORK FOR HERB SCHLOSSER?   WHO? I DON'T RECALL ANYONE BY THAT NAME.

COME NOW, MISS JENKINS, FOR THE LAST TWELVE YEARS YOU WERE HIS PER..   I DON'T KNOW HIM, I TELL YOU! LEAVE ME ALONE!

FOR MORE ON THE STORY, WE HAVE THIS REPORT FROM SIBERIA.   SPRING COMES LATE TO THE URAL MOUNTAINS..

".. AND I'M OUTRAGED," SAYS REP. LACEY DAVENPORT, "THAT THE COMMITTEE HAS REFUSED TO MOVE FORTHRIGHTLY ON THE KOREAN PAYOFF SCANDAL!"

ISN'T THAT INCREDIBLE, ZONKER? THIRTY CONGRESSMEN IMPLICATED, AND STILL NO HEARINGS OR DISCIPLINARY ACTION!

HMM.. MAYBE THEY'RE ALL INNOCENT.

IS IT TRUE YOU GREW UP NEAR DISNEYLAND, ZONKER?

YUP. I USED TO COMMUTE.

YOU KNOW, Z, I'D REALLY LIKE TO GET THE STORY ON THIS KOREAN SCAM. I WONDER IF I COULD GET LACEY DAVENPORT ON MY RADIO SHOW..

YOU KNOW HER?

UH-HUH. I MET HER AT REUNIONS WHILE BARTENDING A COUPLE YEARS AGO..

YEAH, I THINK I'LL GIVE HER A CALL. I'LL BET MY LISTENERS WOULD GIVE ANYTHING TO HEAR WHAT'S REALLY GOING ON IN THE HOUSE ETHICS COMMITTEE, YOU KNOW?

YOU KNOW?

WHILE YOU'RE AT IT, WHY DON'T YOU READ THEM THE PHONE BOOK?

WHAT'D LACEY SAY, MARK?

SHE AGREED TO DO THE INTERVIEW! I'M GOING TO FLY TO WASHINGTON TONIGHT!

WHAT? YOU'RE GOING ALL THE WAY DOWN THERE?

WELL, OF COURSE! FOR A LIVE REMOTE! I'LL JUST HOOK THE MIKE UP TO A PHONE, AND YOU CAN ANCHOR THE SHOW FROM BACK HERE.

ME? NOW, WAIT A MINUTE, MARK! THAT'S PUBLIC AFFAIRS! I CAN'T HANDLE A PUBLIC AFFAIRS SHOW, MAN!

SURE YOU CAN! WHY CAN'T YOU?

FOR CRYING OUT LOUD, MARK! I DON'T EVEN KNOW WHO'S PRESIDENT!

NEITHER DOES ANYONE ELSE. YOU'RE IN TUNE WITH THE TIMES.

I CERTAINLY APPRECIATE YOUR FINDING THE TIME TO TALK TO ME, MRS. D!

WELL, IT'S ALWAYS LOVELY TO SEE YOU, DEAR. I LOOK FORWARD TO OUR LITTLE CHAT..

HI, HO! WHO'S THIS?

DICK, YOU REMEMBER MARK SLACKMEYER, DON'T YOU? FROM THE CAMPUS RADIO STATION?

OH, SURE, I REMEMBER. GOOD TO SEE YOU AGAIN, SON!

THANK YOU, SIR.

I SUPPOSE YOU'RE HERE ABOUT THOSE DREARY LITTLE ORIENTALS.

UH..

IT'S BEEN A LONG WINTER, DEAR. WHY DON'T WE ALL SIT DOWN?

LACEY, FOR SOME TIME, YOUR COMMITTEE HAS BEEN WAITING TO HEAR THE TESTIMONY OF FORMER KOREAN AMBASSADOR KIM. DO YOU THINK KIM'S COOPERATION COULD GET THE INVESTIGATION BACK ON TRACK?

YES, BUT YOU SEE, DEAR, IT'S NOT REALLY THE INVESTIGATION THAT'S BEEN LAGGING. WHY, WE HAVE LOADS OF EVIDENCE!

WHAT IS LACKING IS THE COMMITTEE'S MOTIVATION TO ACT ON THE ALLEGATIONS. SINCE CONGRESS HAS NO INTENTION OF TAKING STRONG MEASURES, IT'S BECOME JUST A QUESTION OF HOW TO PUT ON THE BEST FACE.

A PUBLIC RELATIONS PROBLEM?

RIGHT. IN FACT, WE'RE ALL THINKING OF GOING TO CHINA.

MRS. DAVENPORT, I WONDER IF YOU COULD COMMENT ON THE LAVISH PARTIES THROWN BY KOREAN BUSINESSMAN PARK FOR HOUSE SPEAKER TIP O'NEILL.

WELL, DEAR, I WOULDN'T MAKE TOO MUCH OF THAT. YOU SEE, TIP'S A VERY POPULAR MAN, AND PEOPLE SIMPLY LIKE TO DO THINGS FOR HIM..

FOR INSTANCE, SOME BANKING PALS OF HIS ONCE OFFERED HIM A FREE INTEREST IN A NURSING HOME. RATHER THAN OFFEND HIS FRIENDS OVER A SILLY PRINCIPLE, HE GRACIOUSLY ACCEPTED.

JUST LETS PEOPLE WALK ALL OVER HIM, EH?

QUITE RIGHT. HE JUST DOESN'T SEEM TO KNOW HOW TO SAY NO!

WELL, LISTENERS, THERE YOU HAVE IT! PORTRAIT OF A COVER-UP! ARE YOU INCENSED BY IT? ARE YOU WONDERING WHAT YOU COULD DO TO MAKE LACEY'S JOB EASIER?

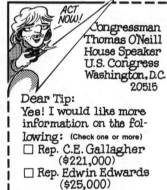

WELL, AS A PUBLIC SERVICE, **WBBY** RADIO HAS TAKEN OUT A COUPON AD IN YOUR LOCAL PAPER—JUST LIKE THE ONES THE GUN NUTS USE! SO IF YOU'RE MAD, CLIP THE COUPON! PASTE IT ON A POSTCARD, AND MAIL WITHOUT DELAY!

ACT NOW!

Congressman
Thomas O'Neill
House Speaker
U.S. Congress
Washington, D.C.
20515

Dear Tip:
Yes! I would like more information on the following: (Check one or more)
☐ Rep. C.E. Gallagher ($221,000)
☐ Rep. Edwin Edwards ($25,000)
☐ Rep. Wm. Minshall ($31,000)

☐ Rep. N. Galifianakis ($10,500)
☐ Rep. John J. McFall ($4,000)
☐ 25 Other Representatives ($?)
☐ 6 Senators ($?)
☐ Yourself ($6,000 in parties)
Hold public hearings now!
Yours for a Clean Congress,

Name
Address

WELL, MRS. D, I'D LIKE TO THANK YOU ONCE AGAIN FOR BEING TODAY'S "PROFILE ON PARADE."

WELL, IT WAS MY PLEASURE, MARK.

I'M SURE I SPEAK FOR ALL MY LISTENERS WHEN I WISH YOU THE BEST OF LUCK IN YOUR EFFORTS TO FLUSH THE BUMS OUT!

THANK YOU VERY MUCH.

WELL, THAT ABOUT WRAPS IT UP DOWN HERE IN THE NATION'S CAPITAL! BACK TO YOU, ZONKER!

UH.. ZONKER?

NOT SO FAST, FELLAH! I ORDERED **ANCHOVIES**, NOT SAUSAGE!

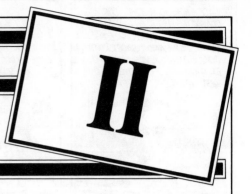

THE FALL OF MALIBU

Q: Tell us about Zonker's beach.

A: Well, technically, it's not really his beach. It's simply named after him. The Zonker Harris Memorial Beach. It was one of the private Malibu beaches recently liberated by the California Coastal Commission.[1] The residents were, of course, furious, and the redwood sign marking the access route was vandalized within twenty-four hours.

[1]Don Neuwirth, the project manager, told the *Los Angeles Times* that beach access in Malibu was a victory for the public. "If you take a picture of us erecting the sign," he said, "try to make it look like the raising of the flag at Iwo Jima."

ZONKER?.. IT'S ME, CORNELL. YOUR DAD CALLED ME WITH THE NEWS..

I'M REAL SORRY TO HEAR ABOUT THE TANNING CLINICS, ZONK, I REALLY AM.

THANKS, MAN, I APPRECIATE THAT..

WERE YOU GOING FOR IT THIS YEAR, Z? WERE YOU ON A HOT ROLL?

ARE YOU KIDDING? I WAS ONE SHADE AWAY FROM QUALIFYING FOR THE GEORGE HAMILTON COPPERTONE PRO-AM CELEBRITY COCOA BUTTER OPEN!

ARE YOU KIDDING? LET ME SEE..

IT DOESN'T SHOW NOW. I'M TOO UPSET..

I APPRECIATE YOUR DROPPING BY, OL' SCHOOLCHUM, BUT I'M AFRAID YOUR SYMPATHY CAN'T HELP ME NOW..

I COULD HAVE BEEN THE BEST, CORNELL. I COULD HAVE BEEN A CONTENDER. THE GEORGE HAMILTON COCOA BUTTER OPEN WAS WITHIN REACH. IT'S THE END OF A DREAM..

WHERE WILL YOU GO, ZONKER? WHAT WILL YOU DO WITH YOUR LIFE NOW?

I DUNNO, MAN, I JUST DUNNO. MAYBE DENTISTRY..

DENTISTRY?

SOMEHOW I'LL JUST HAVE TO START PICKING UP THE PIECES..

WHAT IS IT, KID?

I'VE GOT SOME PURCHASE ORDERS FOR YOU TO SIGN, MR. DUKE..

OH.. THANKS. WHO ARE YOU, ANYWAY?

RILEY, SIR. I'M YOUR NEW ASSISTANT.

ASSISTANT? I DIDN'T ASK FOR ANY ASSISTANT!

I WOULDN'T KNOW, SIR. I WAS JUST TOLD TO REPORT TO YOU.

YOU'RE A NARC, RIGHT, RILEY?

NO, SIR. THE OWNER'S NEPHEW. MAY I HAVE THE AFTERNOON OFF?

SIR, I UNDERSTAND YOU'RE DEVELOPING A NEW SPORTS MEDICINE PROGRAM..

THAT'S RIGHT, RILEY. THE WAY I SEE IT, THE REDSKINS DESERVE THE BEST.

WHEN A PLAYER GOES OUT ONTO THAT FIELD, I BELIEVE HE HAS EVERY RIGHT TO EXPECT CHEMICAL PARITY WITH THE OPPOSING TEAM!

WOW.. WHAT A RESPONSIBILITY!

YOU BETTER BELIEVE IT.

WHAT CAN I DO TO HELP, BOSS?

WELL, I SUPPOSE YOU COULD STAND LOOKOUT.

JOAN, I'VE BEEN LOOKING INTO YOUR REDRESS OPTIONS, DEAR..

AND?

WELL, THE PROBLEM IS THAT YOU'RE BEING DENIED FAIR SALARY AS A HOUSE EMPLOYEE WORKING FOR THE ETHICS COMMITTEE..

THIS I KNOW.

YES, BUT WHAT YOU PROBABLY **DON'T** KNOW IS WHO ARBITRATES SUCH COMPLAINTS!

YOU'RE ABOUT TO TELL ME THAT IT'S THE ETHICS COMMITTEE.

AT LEAST YOU'VE MET EVERYONE.

YEAH, BUT IT TOOK TWO YEARS.

G B Trudeau

THIS CERTAINLY IS A KNOTTY PROBLEM FOR YOU, DEAR. THE PRECEDENTS FOR YOUR CASE ARE SO SCANTY..

YOU KNOW WHAT I'D DO IF I WERE YOU, DEAR? I'D CALL UP A TOP LAW FIRM AND PUT A FULL COMPLEMENT OF ATTORNEYS ON RESEARCH! THEN I'D HIRE A TEAM OF..

LACEY..

NO.. NO, WAIT A MINUTE. THAT WOULDN'T WORK FOR YOU, WOULD IT?

I'M AFRAID NOT.

I KEEP FORGETTING YOU'RE NOT INDEPENDENTLY WEALTHY.

SO DOES MY BUTCHER.

G B Trudeau

YES, THIS IS MRS. DAVENPORT.

MA'AM, I'M CALLING FROM ACCOUNTING WITH THE INFORMATION YOU REQUESTED..

YOUR HUNCH ABOUT THAT YOUNG LAWYER WAS RIGHT. HIS SALARY WAS INCORRECTLY PROGRAMMED IN THE COMPUTER. WE'VE READJUSTED IT DOWN TO HIS PROPER SCALE. I HOPE HE WON'T BE TOO INCONVENIENCED..

NO, NO, I'M SURE NOT. YOU CAUGHT IT EARLY. THANKS VERY MUCH..

OF COURSE, **ANY** KIND OF CONDO IS A TERRIFIC INVESTMENT THESE DAYS!

I'M SURE YOU MADE THE RIGHT DECISION, WOODY.

I SUPPOSE YOU HEARD THE COMPUTER PICKED UP THE DISCREPANCY IN OUR SALARIES..

YES, I DID, WOODY. LACEY JUST CALLED. I HOPE YOU DON'T BLAME ME..!

NO, NO, IT'S NOT YOUR FAULT. IT WOULD HAVE HAPPENED SOONER OR LATER.

I HAVE TO ADMIT, THOUGH, I'M PRETTY SHOCKED..

WHY? DON'T YOU THINK IT WAS FAIR?

YEAH, BUT I CAN'T GET OVER HOW **QUICKLY** JUSTICE WAS SERVED!

WELL, THOSE COMPUTERS TODAY ARE PRETTY AMAZING..

G B Trudeau

..AND IT HAS TO BE SOMETHING REALLY SPECIAL. SOMETHING I CAN TREASURE ALWAYS..

WELL, HOW ABOUT THESE DIET PILLS, HONEY? EXACT REPLICAS OF ELVIS' PERSONAL PRESCRIPTION!

WOW..NO FOOLING?

UH-HUH. AND THEY'RE PRICED SPECIALLY. THEY'VE BEEN MARKED DOWN TO A LOW $5.

MARKED DOWN? YOU MARKED DOWN ELVIS' PERSONAL DIET PILLS?

THAT'S RIGHT! WHILE THEY LAST!

BUT THAT'S AWFUL! HOW COULD YOU CHEAPEN ELVIS' MEMORY LIKE THAT?

LOOK, HONEY, WE GOTTA MAKE ROOM FOR THE FALL LINE!

..AND I GET IN AT 2:30! YOU'LL MEET ME, WON'T YOU, BABY?

YEAH, I GUESS. HOW WAS GRACELAND?

OH, IT WAS SO BEAUTIFUL, B.D.! I WISH YOU COULD HAVE SEEN IT! THE GRAVE IS UNDER A BUNCH OF GREEK COLUMNS, AND IT'S COVERED WITH FLOWERS FROM FANS!

AND THE MANSION, YOU CAN'T BELIEVE THE MANSION! ESPECIALLY AT NIGHT! IT WAS ALL SO MOVING I NEARLY CRIED.

UH-HUH. DID YOU PICK UP A POSTCARD OR SOMETHING?

OR SOMETHING, YES.

"ELVIS ARON PRESLEY.. A LIVING LEGEND IN HIS OWN TIME.."

ISN'T IT BEAUTIFUL, B.D.?

"A LIVING LEGEND IN HIS OWN TIME"? ISN'T THAT A TAD REDUNDANT?

OH, C'MON, READ THE REST OF IT..

"HE REVOLUTIONIZED THE FIELD OF MUSIC AND WON ITS HIGHEST AWARDS.." BOOPSIE, WHAT IS THIS, HIS PRESS AGENT'S EULOGY?

NO, NO, IT'S AN EXACT REPLICA OF ELVIS' GRAVESTONE.

YOU'RE KIDDING.

WELL, EXCEPT FOR THE LITTLE THERMOMETER.

WHAT IS IT, RILEY?

SIR, JOE THE TRAINER WANTS TO SEE YOU..

WHAT ABOUT?

EDDIE JUST GOT WIPED OUT ON A BLINDSIDE BLOCK. HE LOOKS PRETTY HURT.

WHAT AM I SUPPOSED TO DO ABOUT IT? TRADE HIM IN THE MIDDLE OF A GAME?

THE DOCTOR'S CAUGHT IN TRAFFIC. JOE SAYS YOU'RE A LICENSED PHYSICIAN.

QUITE RIGHT.

SHOULD I BOIL SOME WATER OR SOMETHING, SIR?

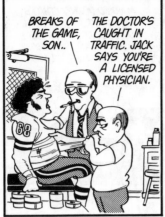

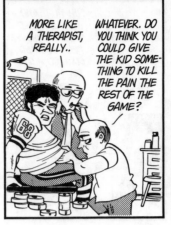

MR. REDFERN? YO?

IT'S ME. DON'T TURN AROUND. THEY MIGHT BE WATCHING. WHO?

THE NFL. I'M HERE AT GREAT PERSONAL RISK. MINE IS A TALE RIFE WITH SCANDAL AND INTRIGUE. NOT TO MENTION MELODRAMA. MAYBE YOU BETTER ORDER FIRST.

RIGHT. HOW ARE THE CHEESEBURGERS? THEY CAN BE TRUSTED.

..AND BOTH QUARTERBACKS ARE NOW OUT FOR THE REST OF THE SEASON! WELL, THAT'S QUITE A STORY, KID. I'LL HAVE TO CHECK IT OUT, OF COURSE..

TAKE YOUR TIME, MR. REDFERN. THE PROBLEM ISN'T GOING AWAY TOMORROW. WHAT TIME HAVE YOU GOT? OH..IT'S ABOUT ONE.

OKAY, I GOTTA GO. HERE'S WHAT I WANT YOU TO DO. ORDER THE APRICOT FLAMBÉ. WHEN THE WAITER STARTS TO LIGHT IT, KNOCK HIS ARM SO THAT THE BRANDY SPILLS ALL OVER THE TABLE..

AS THE FLAMES SPREAD TO THE TABLECLOTH, I'LL SLIP OUT IN THE CONFUSION. KID, DO YOU COME HERE OFTEN?

CLACKITY! RUUMMBLE! CLACKITY! WHIPPITY! WHIP!

EXTRA! INSIDER, 15, RAPS 'SKINS IN SPEED SCANDAL!

SPORTS
MONDA

DrugDoc
Termed
'Menace
To Sport'
By Richard Redfern
WASHINGTON—An Int

RING! RING! GET THAT, WILL YA, KID? I WONDER IF WE COULD TALK FIRST, SIR..

IT'S ALL THERE, DUKE—THE DRUGS, THE INJURIES, EVERYTHING! MY PHONE HASN'T STOPPED RINGING SINCE THE EARLY EDITION HIT THE STREETS!

DAMN! THIS COULD BE WORSE THAN THE STOLEN PLAYBOOK! HOW THE HELL DID THE "POST" FIND OUT, COACH? EDDIE'S THE ONLY ONE BESIDES US WHO KNOWS ABOUT IT, AND HE'S IN A COMA!

I DON'T KNOW, DUKE, BUT IF YOU DON'T TRACK THE LITTLE SNITCH DOWN FAST, YOU MIGHT AS WELL START PACKING! TROUBLE, SIR?

IT JUST CAME TO ME, COACH. IT WASN'T MY FAULT, SIR. THEY PLIED ME WITH CHEESEBURGERS.

YOUR FOOTBALL ARTICLE SEEMS TO BE CAUSING QUITE A STIR, RICHARD..

YEAH, THAT GUY DUKE SURE DOESN'T TAKE THINGS LYING DOWN.

HE RELEASED A 2,000 WORD REBUTTAL YESTERDAY, AND TODAY HE'S HOLDING A PRESS CONFERENCE IN HIS OFFICE..

HE CLAIMS HE'S EVEN GOING TO PRODUCE THE INJURED PLAYER TO TESTIFY ON HIS BEHALF!

I DUNNO, SIR, HE DOESN'T LOOK SO GOOD..

NURSE! CUT THIS MAN DOWN!

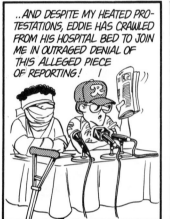

..AND DESPITE MY HEATED PRO-TESTATIONS, EDDIE HAS CRAWLED FROM HIS HOSPITAL BED TO JOIN ME IN OUTRAGED DENIAL OF THIS ALLEGED PIECE OF REPORTING!

THIS ARTICLE REPRESENTS THE SHODDIEST KIND OF JOURNALISM! NAMES, DATES, PLACES ARE **ALL** INACCURATE! EVEN DOSAGES ARE DISTORTED AND TAKEN TOTALLY OUT OF CONTEXT!

AS EDDIE VIGOROUSLY CONFIRMS, THE "CONTROLLED SUBSTANCES" I GAVE HIM IN LAST SUNDAY'S GAME WERE NOTHING MORE THAN COMMON ASPIRIN TABLETS! RIGHT, EDDIE?

MMPHH.

NOW, I HOPE WE'VE HEARD THE LAST OF THIS SILLY EPISODE!

>WHEEZE!< COUGH! COUGH!

WHILE WE'RE ALL HERE, I'D LIKE TO TAKE THE OPPORTUN-ITY TO COMMENT FURTHER ON RED-FERN'S INFLAMMATORY PROSE..

UNNH..

IT IS A SORRY STATE OF AFFAIRS WHEN A POLITI-CAL REPORTER IS SENT TO COVER FOOTBALL, A SUB-JECT HE IS CLEARLY UN-EQUIPPED TO COMMENT ON!

UNNH.. ARRGH!

OBVIOUSLY, IN FOOTBALL PEOPLE GET HURT! BUT IT IS THE RISK OF INJURY THAT MAKES THE GAME GREAT! IT IS THE COURAGE OF ATH-LETES AS THEY..

BONK!

EDDIE, WILL YOU SETTLE DOWN? THIS IS IMPORTANT.

>CHIRP!< CAW! CAW!

>RIBBIT! RIBBIT!<

GOOD EVENING. I'M ROLAND BUR-TON HEDLEY, JR., AND THAT WAS THE SCENE TODAY AT CAMP DAVID, SITE OF JIMMY CARTER'S DAZ-ZLING MIDEAST SUMMITRY!

WHAT REALLY WENT ON DURING THOSE THIRTEEN DAYS IN SEPTEM-BER? JOIN US AS ABC WIDE WORLD OF NEWS TAKES AN IN-DEPTH LOOK AT.. **CABIN FEVER!**

"CABIN FEVER: FOOTPATHS TO GLORY," BROUGHT TO YOU BY..

>CHIRP!< TWITTER!<

CABIN FEVER
abc Wide World Special Report

CABIN FEVER. FOR THIRTEEN LONG DAYS, IT HELD THE WORLD IN ITS GRIP.

WHAT WENT ON IN THOSE SMALL BUT ATTRACTIVELY APPOINTED COTTAGES AT CAMP DAVID? ABC WIDE WORLD OF NEWS RE-CREATES THE ACTION!

DAY ONE. IT'S A LAZY, WARM AFTERNOON AS PRESIDENT ANWAR SADAT'S HELICOPTER TOUCHES DOWN AT CAMP DAVID..

ROLLIE?

YES, FRANK REYNOLDS IN WASHINGTON. YOU'D LIKE TO ADD SOMETHING?

AS I RECALL, THE MOOD WAS HOPEFUL. BACK TO YOU.

DAY FIVE. THE ISRAELIS CLIMB TO NEW HEIGHTS OF INFLEXIBILITY. BEGIN'S INTRANSIGENCE HANGS OVER THE CAMP LIKE A WET BLANKET.

STILL, OCCASIONAL LEVITY CUTS THROUGH THE GLOOM. DURING AN EARLY MORNING STROLL, BEGIN REMARKS TO CARTER, "THIS PLACE IS LIKE HEAVEN ON EARTH."

THE PRESIDENT, SENSING AN OPENING, OFFERS HIM CAMP DAVID. BEGIN, SENSING A RETIREMENT HOME, ACCEPTS.

IF ONLY FOR A MOMENT, CAMP DAVID RINGS WITH LAUGHTER.

DAY TEN. THE MARCH TOWARD PEACE FLOUNDERS. AS TEMPERS FLARE AND ANTES ARE UPPED, JIMMY CARTER ACTS. A TOP AMERICAN NEGOTIATOR REMEMBERS.

WELL, HE SCHEDULED A MOVIE, "PATTON." IT WAS A RATHER COURAGEOUS ACT OF PROGRAMING, SINCE THE SAME FILM ONCE INSPIRED NIXON TO INVADE CAMBODIA.

THE EFFECT WAS QUITE DIFFERENT ON THE ISRAELIS, THOUGH. AFTER ONE ESPECIALLY GORY SCENE, DEFENSE MINISTER WEIZMAN ROSE AND CRIED OUT, "NEVER AGAIN!" THE IMPASSE WAS BROKEN.

COMING UP: PEACE ON THE RAMPAGE.

AMERICAN NEGOTIATOR, IN YOUR OWN WORDS, DESCRIBE THE MOOD AS DAY THIRTEEN BROKE AT CAMP DAVID. IT WAS ONE OF UNCERTAINTY, WAS IT NOT?

THAT'S RIGHT, ROLAND. EVEN AFTER THE CLIMACTIC SADAT-CARTER MEETING IN ASPEN LODGE, THE SUCCESS OF THE SUMMIT WAS STILL IN DOUBT..

AS SADAT WAS LEAVING HIS CABIN, HE BUMPED INTO THE ISRAELI PRIME MINISTER. OFFERING HIS HAND, HE SMILED AND SAID, "LET US BEGIN, BEGIN."

AND BEGIN REPLIED?

"WE'RE NOT OUT OF THE WOODS YET."

STILL DOTTING THE "i"'S, EH?

..AND WITH THE RESTORATION OF THE SINAI CAME THE RETURN OF VITAL OIL FIELDS. IN ECONOMIC TERMS, IT WAS A SIGNIFICANT CONCESSION!

REMEMBER, LANGUAGE WAS REALLY THE KEY TO THE NEGOTIATIONS. EACH SIDE HAD ITS OWN TERMINOLOGY FOR DESCRIBING A GIVEN GEO-POLITICAL SITUATION.

FOR INSTANCE, MR. SADAT KEPT REFERRING TO THE WEST BANK AS AN "INADMISSIBLY OCCUPIED TERRITORY."

AND MR. BEGIN?

BEGIN CALLED IT "THE LAND OF MILK AND HONEY."

DAIRY PRODUCTS? THAT'S A NEW TWIST, ISN'T IT?

TOP AMERICAN NEGOTIATOR, IT WASN'T ALL PEACHES AND CREAM AT CAMP DAVID, WAS IT? IN FACT, YOU HAD YOUR SHARE OF LOW WATER MARKS, RIGHT?

THAT'S RIGHT, ROLAND, I'D SAY THE WORST MOMENT CAME WHEN BEGIN ACCUSED SADAT OF DELIBERATELY ATTACKING ISRAELIS WORSHIPED FOR YOM KIPPUR IN 1973.

HOW DID SADAT RESPOND?

AT FIRST, WITH SOME DIFFICULTY.

AND THEN?

THEN HE ACCUSED BEGIN OF TRYING TO LAY A GUILT TRIP ON HIM.

DOES SEEM LIKE A BIT OF A CHEAP SHOT..

DAY 15: CAMP DAVID PLUS TWO. THE HISTORIC PEACE ACCORDS KINDLE AN OUTPOURING OF PUBLIC ACCLAIM!

FOR CARTER, SUCCESS IS SWEET. HIS STANDING WITH CONGRESS AND WITH THE AMERICAN PEOPLE HAS NEVER BEEN ON FIRMER GROUND.

CASE IN POINT: IN THE WAKE OF CAMP DAVID, A NEW POLL REVEALS THAT 93% OF THE PUBLIC NOW FEELS THAT PRESIDENT CARTER IS DOING AN EXCELLENT JOB FIGHTING INFLATION.

MOREOVER, 86% NOW APPROVE OF HIS HANDLING OF THE LANCE AFFAIR..

WELL, I ALWAYS HAVE.

ME, TOO. HE'S BEEN JUST GREAT!

DAY 16. BEFORE MR. BEGIN DEPARTS FOR HOME, HE GRANTS AN EXCLUSIVE INTERVIEW TO ABC NEWS. HE IS ASKED IF HE HAS ANY PLANS FOR TAKING A VACATION..

ABSOLUTELY NOT! AS I TOLD NBC YESTERDAY, THE STRUGGLE FOR US NEVER ENDS. THE JEWISH PEOPLE MUST NEVER LET DOWN THEIR GUARD AGAINST THE ENEMY!

WE HAVE SUFFERED FOR TOO LONG, WE HAVE ENDURED PERSECUTION, HORRIBLE WARS, AND THE THREAT OF EXTINCTION FOR OVER TWO THOUSAND YEARS, BEGINNING WITH..

ABC NEWS WITHDREW THE QUESTION. BACK AFTER THIS..

WHAT DO THE NEW ACCORDS SPELL FOR MR. BEGIN'S CAREER? IN A FAR-RANGING INTERVIEW, I ASKED THE DOUR LITTLE EX-TERRORIST ABOUT HIS POLITICAL FUTURE..

WELL, AS I TOLD CBS EARLIER, MR. HEDLEY, SOME FRIENDS WILL CRITICIZE ME. BUT THAT IS THEIR RIGHT. IT IS TO BE EXPECTED. THERE IS A PHILOSOPHICAL EXPRESSION FOR THIS..

SWITCHING FROM ENGLISH, MR. BEGIN THEN SPOKE DIRECTLY TO HIS OWN PEOPLE..

.."C'EST LA VIE."

CABIN FEVER PLUS TWO WEEKS. THE DRAMA COMES TO A CLOSE..

THE TWO WEEKS OF DAY-AND-NIGHT SUMMITRY FINALLY CATCH UP WITH AN EXHAUSTED PRESIDENT..

TAKING THE EVENING OFF, MR. CARTER HEADS OUT TO RFK STADIUM, WHERE HE IS THE HONORED GUEST OF THE MANAGEMENT OF THE WASHINGTON REDSKINS FOOTBALL CLUB..

JUST COFFEE. WHY?

FOR THIRTEEN STRAIGHT DAYS? C'MON, SIR, YOU CAN TELL ME!

HEY, KIRBY! WHY THE LONG FACE?

I'M AT ODDS WITH MY ERA, ZONKER.

OF COURSE, YOU ARE, KIRBY. WHAT ARE YOU TALKING ABOUT?

GROWING UP IN THE SEVENTIES. I CAN'T SEEM TO ATTACH ANY MEANING TO IT..

HERE WE ARE, ALMOST NINE YEARS INTO THE DECADE, AND THE MAJOR CULTURAL CONTRIBUTION OF THE SEVENTIES IS A FIFTIES REVIVAL CRAZE!

OH, C'MON, KIRBY! WHAT ABOUT DISCO? AND WATERGATE BOOKS?!

WELL, OKAY, BUT HOW MANY OTHER BRIGHT SPOTS WERE THERE?

I DON'T QUITE UNDERSTAND, KIRBY. WHAT EXACTLY IS WRONG WITH THE SEVENTIES?

THEY LACK DEFINITION, Z. I DON'T FEEL LIKE I LIVE IN AN ERA I CAN REALLY CALL MY OWN!

OH, I'VE SHOPPED AROUND, OF COURSE. I'VE CHECKED OUT ALL THE TOP-GROSSING PERIOD FILMS, "GREASE," "ANIMAL HOUSE," "COMING HOME," ETC., BUT NONE OF THEM IS REALLY ME. I GUESS YOU COULD SAY I'M A PEG IN SEARCH OF A HOLE!

ROUND OR SQUARE?

DOESN'T MATTER. AS LONG AS IT CAN SUPPORT THE WEIGHT OF MY CONVICTIONS.

BOY, YOU REALLY ARE DEPRESSED..

DO YOU REALIZE I HAVE ABSOLUTELY NO MEMORY OF THE FORD YEARS?

VIRGINIA REEL

Q: One of the things that greeted Senator-elect John Warner and his wife, Elizabeth, upon their arrival in the Capital was a series on them in *Doonesbury,* an event which earned its author the censure of the G.O.P. Caucus of the Virginia General Assembly.[1] Any comment?

A: Sure. Better late than never. I had always assumed that the State of Virginia would spare itself the embarrassment of sending the Warners to Washington, but I'm as hopeless a handicapper as I am an optimist. Having missed the boat, I settled for a recap of some of the highlights of the campaign.[2] From the beginning, Warner's deployment of his assets, which is to say his wife and his money, was an absolute marvel, although losing the primary, as he somehow managed to do, was one of those things which gives opportunism a bad name. Fortunately, Providence interceded. His opponent was killed in an airplane crash, and John redeemed himself by immediately volunteering to replace him. Talk about your early bird...

[1]According to the AP, the motion's sponsor, State Senator Wiley Mitchell, announced, "I don't think we should sit placidly by and let the gnomes of the world run over us without expressing indignation."

[2]Warner later told the *Washington Post,* "The facts in the strip are totally false and inaccurate. Oh, I'm not going to pick them out. The people of Virginia know the facts."

You are cordially invited to a Media Event in honor of Senator and Mrs. Elizabeth Taylor

GOOD GOD, HONEY! DO YOU HAVE ANY IDEA HOW **EARLY** IT IS?

YES, SIR, BUT IT COULDN'T WAIT..

I'M JUST ABOUT TO GO INTO MY FOREIGN POLICY SEMINAR WITH PROFESSOR KISSINGER! I NEED YOUR ADVICE..

MY ADVICE? ON WHAT?

WELL, ON WHAT SORTS OF THINGS I SHOULD OR SHOULDN'T BRING UP IN CLASS.

WHAT'D YOU HAVE IN MIND?

WELL, LIKE, IS HE STILL SENSITIVE ABOUT BEING A WAR CRIMINAL?

HELL, NO! HE'S **USED** TO BEING KIDDED ABOUT IT!

TELL ME, FELLOW STUDENTS, IS THERE ANYTHING SPECIAL I SHOULD KNOW ABOUT PROFESSOR KISSINGER?

NOT REALLY. JUST TRY NOT TO TAKE HIM TOO SERIOUSLY. GOD KNOWS **WE** DON'T.

I'M TOLD HE HAS A WONDERFUL SENSE OF HUMOR, THAT HE'S ALWAYS QUIPPING AND TELLING JOKES.

HENRY? JOKES AND QUIPS?

YEAH, LIKE THE ONE HE TELLS ABOUT WANTING TO BE "BORN AGAIN," ONLY THIS TIME IN THE U.S. SO HE'D QUALIFY FOR THE PRESIDENCY!

I'M AFRAID THAT'S NO JOKE, MISS.

IT'S NOT? BUT I WAS TOLD IT WAS HYSTERICAL.

GOOD MORNING. IN TODAY'S READING..

DOC! WHERE ARE YOUR MANNERS? WE HAVE A NEW CLASSMATE!

WHAT'S THAT, MR. WEINBERGER?

SAY HELLO TO MS. HUAN, DOC! FRESH OFF THE BOAT FROM THE PEOPLE'S REPUBLIC!

WELCOME TO OUR CLASS, MS. HUAN. IN LIGHT OF THE RECENT INITIATIVES BETWEEN OUR TWO NATIONS, IT IS A SPECIAL HONOR.

FOR ME AS WELL, SIR! IT IS A FELICITOUS AND HISTORIC TURN WHICH OUR MINGLED DESTINIES HAVE TAKEN!

IT IS INDEED. NOW, IN TODAY'S READING..

I HOPE YOU'LL LET ME BUY YOU A DRINK AFTER CLASS, SIR.

ALTHOUGH THE RECOGNITION OF CHINA IS A GREAT STEP FORWARD, IT SHOULD BE NOTED THAT THE TERMS TO WHICH CARTER AGREED ARE **IDENTICAL** TO THOSE OFFERED FOUR YEARS EARLIER!

BUT, DR. KISSINGER, COULDN'T THE SAME THING BE SAID ABOUT YOUR 1973 VIETNAM CEASE-FIRE ACCORDS?

NO, MISS HUAN, THE TWO ARE **NOT**..

NOT COMPARABLE. YOU'RE RIGHT, SIR. FORGIVE ME, I'D LIKE TO BACK OFF THAT ANALOGY.

YOU WOULD?

YES, SIR. I WAS JUST TESTING THE LIMITS OF YOUR AUTHORITY. CARRY ON.

ANYTHING FOR ME FROM THE AUDUBON SOCIETY, DEAREST?

NO..NO, IT LOOKS LIKE NOTHING BUT BILLS.

BILLS? THEY CERTAINLY DON'T WASTE ANY TIME ONCE CHRISTMAS IS OVER, DO THEY?

NO, THEY DON'T..OH, HERE'S AN INVITATION!

"YOU ARE CORDIALLY INVITED TO A SMALL MEDIA EVENT HONORING SENATOR AND MRS. ELIZABETH TAYLOR.."

TO WHAT?

HOW EXCITING! WE'VE BEEN ASKED TO THE OPENING SALVO!

WHO?

BUT, DEAREST! IT'S THE VERY FIRST PARTY FOR ELIZABETH TAYLOR AND HER CONSORT!

I'M SORRY, LACEY, YOU'LL JUST HAVE TO GO BY YOURSELF..

I'VE GOT BETTER THINGS TO DO THAN GO ALL THE WAY ACROSS TOWN JUST TO MEET THE WIFE OF SOME DIM DILETTANTE WHO MANAGED TO BUY, MARRY AND LUCK HIS WAY INTO THE U.S. SENATE!

BUT, SWEETEST! I HAVE TO GO! THEY'RE REPUBLICANS!

WELL, I DON'T SEE HOW THAT'S OUR FAULT. THAT'S THE TROUBLE WITH THE G.O.P.— ANYBODY CAN JOIN!

OH, C'MON, DICK, JUST THIS ONCE. THEN WE'LL IGNORE THEM!

WELL, IF YOU MUST. BUT I'M WAITING IN THE CAR.

NOW, STOP CARRYING ON, DICK! I'M SURE JOHN WARNER GOT TO THE SENATE ON HIS OWN MERITS!

OH, C'MON, LACEY. REMEMBER WHEN THE PARTY'S ORIGINAL NOMINEE DIED IN THAT ACCIDENT?

THE WARNERS WERE SO STRICKEN WITH SYMPATHY THAT THEY OFFERED TO TAKE ON THE CAMPAIGN DEBT AND TO SET UP A TRUST FUND FOR THE FAMILY. GUESS WHO WAS THEN TAPPED THE NEXT DAY?

WELL, THEY DIDN'T HAVE TO OFFER ANYTHING, DICK..

CAN'T YOU JUST HEAR HIM MAKING HIS CASE? "I'LL SHOW YOU MY QUID IF YOU SHOW ME YOUR QUO!"

NOW, DICK, YOU'VE BEEN AROUND POLITICS LONG ENOUGH TO..

TO GROW CYNICAL? NEVER! I'M CONSTANTLY AMAZED!

LACEY! DEAREST! I'VE BEEN LOOKING ALL OVER FOR YOU!

WE JUST ARRIVED, GAIL. SORRY WE'RE SO LATE!

DON'T BE SILLY! I WAS JUST AFRAID YOU WEREN'T COMING..

WELL, AS YOU KNOW, DEAR, I'M NOT WILD ABOUT FILM PEOPLE. BUT LIZ TAYLOR, WELL ..

THRILLING, ISN'T IT? WAIT UNTIL YOU SEE HER! SHE'S..

WE KNOW. "A TAD OVERWEIGHT, BUT WITH VIOLET EYES TO DIE FOR."

WHY, DICK! I THOUGHT YOU JUST GOT HERE!

WE DID. THAT'S FROM ONE OF THEIR BUMPER STICKERS.

MAY I JUST SAY HOW DEEPLY HONORED BOTH OF US ARE TO BE HERE TONIGHT. IT'S THE CULMINATION OF A DREAM!

WE HAD A TOUGH RACE. BUT HAPPILY THE VOTERS OF THE STATE OF VIRGINIA KNEW ME AND THEY KNEW WHAT I STOOD FOR, EVEN WHEN I MYSELF WASN'T SURE.

AS THOSE OF YOU WHO ARE IN POLITICS KNOW, YOU CAN'T BUY THAT KIND OF SUPPORT, ALTHOUGH WE CERTAINLY DID OUR LEVEL BEST!

IT IS THUS WITH GREAT PRIDE THAT I INTRODUCE MY HUSBAND, JOHN WARNER!

WELL DONE! ADMIT IT, DICK, SHE HANDLES HERSELF SUPERBLY!

THANK YOU, ELIZABETH! IF I MAY, I'D LIKE TO MAKE A TOAST TO OUR NEW FRIENDS!

AS YOU KNOW, WE HAD ORIGINALLY INTENDED TO SPEND THE FALL "EATING OUR WAY ACROSS FRANCE," AS ELIZABETH LIKES TO PUT IT..

BUT FATE INTERVENED, DUTY CALLED, AND NOW HERE WE ARE IN WASHINGTON, ATTENDING WONDERFUL PARTIES!

SO LET'S DRINK TO FUTURE PARTIES! AND TO THE SENATE, TOO!

"THE SENATE, TOO?"

YOU WERE RIGHT. HE DOES HAVE A SERIOUS SIDE.

GOOD MORNING, FRONT DESK.

YEAH, THIS IS MR. DUKE. WHERE AM I?

UH..YOU'RE AT THE RAMADA INN IN MIAMI, SIR.

MIAMI? OH, C'MON, WHAT THE HELL WOULD I BE DOING IN MIAMI?

I WOULDN'T KNOW, SIR. MAYBE THE SUPER BOWL. IS EVERYTHING OKAY?

OKAY? ARE YOU GOING TO PRETEND YOU DON'T KNOW THERE'S AN OVERTURNED GOLF CART IN MY BATHROOM?

THIS MUST BE ROOM 402.

LISTEN, THIS PLACE IS FILTHY! I WANT TO CHECK OUT!

IT'S THE BELLBOY, SIR. I'VE GOT THE REST OF YOUR ORDER, SIR..

ORDER? WHAT ORDER?

THE CASE OF GIN, SIR. AND THE GRAPEFRUIT AND THE BADMINTON NETS YOU WANTED!

BADMINTON NETS? I ORDERED BADMINTON NETS?

UH..YES, SIR. YOU SAID YOU WERE CONDUCTING SOME SORT OF EXPERIMENT!

EXPERIMENT? LOOK, I DON'T KNOW WHAT'S GOING ON HERE. JUST SET EVERYTHING BY THE DOOR, OKAY?

OKAY. YOU THROUGH WITH THE GOLF CART YET?

UH.. I'M NOT SURE. I NEED TIME TO PIECE THIS THING TOGETHER..

MR. SECRETARY, THE PEOPLE'S REPUBLIC OF CHINA *VEHEMENTLY* PROTESTS VIETNAM'S *BRUTAL* ARMORED ASSAULT INTO THE SOVEREIGN STATE OF KAMPUCHEA!

HANOI'S VILE AND SAVAGE BLITZKRIEG IS AN *AFFRONT* TO ALL PEACE-LOVING PEOPLES OF THE WORLD, AND SHOULD BE *CONDEMNED* BY THIS COUNCIL AS THE *DESPICABLE*, CRIMINAL ACT THAT IT IS!

AMBASSADOR PHRED, HOW DOES VIETNAM RESPOND?

AMBASSADOR PHRED?

SORRY, MR. SECRETARY, I WASN'T PLUGGED IN. WHAT ARE THE CHARGES AGAIN?

MR. SECRETARY, THIS IS AN *OUTRAGE!* THE AMBASSADOR FROM CHINA HAS NO GROUNDS *WHATSOEVER* FOR HIS CHARGE OF VIETNAMESE IMPERIALISM!

THE HOSTILITIES IN CAMBODIA WERE THE RESULT OF A *POPULAR* UPRISING AGAINST A BRUTAL REGIME! VIETNAM PLAYED ONLY A MINOR ADVISORY ROLE!

ADVISORY, MR. AMBASSADOR? THEN PERHAPS YOU COULD EXPLAIN TO THIS COUNCIL THE 100,000 SOLDIERS THAT POURED ACROSS THE BORDER ON DECEMBER 24!

WELL?

LOOK, THEY HEARD SHOTS. THEY WERE CURIOUS.

PHRED, YOUR DEFENSE TODAY OF VIETNAM'S ACTIONS WAS BRILLIANT, JUST BRILLIANT! I *KNEW* WHEN WE SIGNED THAT FRIENDSHIP ACCORD LAST YEAR YOU'D MAKE US PROUD!

WHY, THANK YOU, MR. AMBASSADOR.

YOU PEOPLE ARE DOING A GREAT JOB FOR US, JUST GREAT! KEEP IT UP!

WHO'S THAT, PHRED?

VIKTOR LOZINSKY, ONE OF OUR SOVIET FRIENDS.

SEEMS NICE.

ACTUALLY, HE'S A PIG, BUT THEY MAKE GREAT TANKS.

PHRED?

MIGUEL! WELCOME BACK! HOW'S EVERYTHING IN MANILA?

TO BE HONEST, PHRED, A BIT TENSE. SPEAKING FOR MY FELLOW DOMINOES, I SHOULD TELL YOU THAT YOUR COUNTRY'S LATEST REAL ESTATE GRAB HAS LEFT ALL OF US A LITTLE JUMPY.

OH, NOW, C'MON, MIGUEL—WITH CHINA CHAFING AT OUR BORDERS, YOU THINK WE NEED THE AGGRAVATION? BESIDES, OUR ASIAN NEIGHBORS ARE VALUED TRADING PARTNERS!

THEN I HAVE YOUR WORD?

WELL, NO, BUT I REALLY THINK YOU'RE BEING PARANOID.

GOOD EVENING. I'M ROLAND HEDLEY BURTON, JR. TONIGHT, ".30/.30" EXAMINES ONE OF THE STRANGEST PHENOMENA IN RECENT POLITICAL HISTORY..

HIS NAME IS EDWARD MOORE KENNEDY. HE IS THE SENIOR SENATOR FROM MASSACHUSETTS. BUT TO HIS THOUSANDS OF DEVOTED FOLLOWERS, HE IS KNOWN SIMPLY AS "TED."

WHO ARE THESE FOLLOWERS? WHERE DO THEY COME FROM? WHAT FORCE DRIVES THEM TO THROW GOOD MONEY AFTER BAD? TONIGHT, ABC WIDE WORLD OF NEWS LOOKS AT..

"THE LIBERAL CULT: THREAT FROM THE LEFT!"

THE LIBERAL CULT. HUMANE. JUST. FREE-SPENDING. AND UNDER THE GUIDANCE OF ITS CHARISMATIC LEADER, "TED", A MYSTERIOUS NEW FORCE ON THE POLITICAL SCENE!

WHO ARE THESE "LIBERALS"? HOW CAN WE ACCOUNT FOR THEIR CURIOUS APPEARANCE IN AN ERA OF FISCAL RESPONSIBILITY? WE ASKED CONSERVATIVE COLUMNIST DIRK DUPONT.

BEATS ME. I THOUGHT WE HAD THE SUCKERS UNDER CONTROL.

COMING UP: A LIBERAL'S MOTHER RECALLS HER SHAME.

WHAT SORT OF PERSON JOINS KENNEDY'S SO-CALLED "CULT OF CONSCIENCE"? WHAT EXACTLY IS A LIBERAL? ANTIOCH SOCIOLOGIST ALVIN RASHBAUM COMMENTS.

WELL, AS FAR AS WE CAN TELL, "TED" DRAWS HIS SUPPORTERS FROM THE RANKS OF PEOPLE WHO'VE NEVER HAD IT SO GOOD—BLACKS, WORKERS, THE ELDERLY, AND, OF COURSE, NEWLY ARRIVED BOAT PEOPLE.

THE TYPICAL LIBERAL FANTASIZES ABOUT BUILDING A JUST AND EGALITARIAN SOCIETY. WHAT HE DOESN'T UNDERSTAND, OF COURSE, IS THAT THESE THINGS COST MONEY.

IS HE DANGEROUS?

ONLY WHEN HE VOTES. HAPPILY, HE'S DISAFFECTED RIGHT NOW.

WHAT SORT OF SWAY DOES "TED" HAVE OVER HIS FOLLOWERS? I ASKED LIBERAL CONGRESSMAN BART SVIGALS, WHO FLED WASHINGTON DURING LAST YEAR'S OUTBREAK OF TAX-CUT FEVER..

CONGRESSMAN, YOU'VE BEEN IN SELF-IMPOSED EXILE NOW FOR OVER A YEAR, RIGHT?

THAT'S CORRECT, ROLLIE. EVER SINCE THE ROTH-KEMP BILL WAS INTRODUCED.

WOULD YOU RETURN TO CONGRESS IF SENATOR KENNEDY ASKED YOU TO?

YES, I WOULD. I WOULD DO ANYTHING FOR THE MAN.

WOULD YOU.. WOULD YOU OVERSPEND FOR HIM?

LAVISHLY. WITHOUT HESITATION.

COMPASSION. JUSTICE. A FAIR SHAKE. THESE ARE THE PROFESSED GOALS OF THE KENNEDY "CULT OF CONSCIENCE."

AND YET, FOR ALL THE EGALITARIAN POSTURING OF THE LIBERALS, GATHERING SIGNS INDICATE THAT WITHIN THE CULT ITSELF, SOME ARE MORE EQUAL THAN OTHERS!

ABC NEWS HAS JUST LEARNED OF THE EXISTENCE OF AN INNER ELITE, A TIGHTLY KNIT CADRE OF LOYALISTS SO CLOSE TO "TED" THAT THEY'RE ACTUALLY RELATED TO HIM.

REFERRED TO AS THE KENNEDY "CLAN," THEIR EXACT NUMBER IS UNKNOWN..

THE KENNEDY "CLAN". HEIRS TO A POWERFUL LIBERAL LEGACY, THEY ASPIRE FANATICALLY TO A STATE OF TOTAL GRACE.

RESTRICTED DURING THE SUMMER MONTHS TO A FAMILY "COMPOUND," CLAN MEMBERS ARE FORCED TO PRACTICE THEIR BACKHANDS, GROW LONG, UNKEMPT HAIR, AND POSE FOR ENDLESS GROUP PHOTOGRAPHS.

LATER, IN THE FALL, YOUNGER CLAN MEMBERS ARE SENT AWAY TO THE RIGORS OF BOARDING SCHOOL, WHILE OLDER MEMBERS ARE CONFINED TO HARVARD.

DISCIPLINE IS TIGHT. ONLY AFTER THEY HAVE COMPLETED THEIR STUDIES MAY THEY RUN FOR OFFICE.

HAM? THE CONTRACTORS ARE HERE TO START WORK ON THE "NEW FOUNDATION."

GOOD! SEND 'EM IN!

MORNIN', MR. JORDAN.

HI! YOU BOYS FROM THE GSA?

UH.. NO, SIR. WE'RE INDEPENDENTS. BUT WE'RE FULLY BONDED.

THAT'S WHAT THEY ALL SAY. YOU HAD ANY EXPERIENCE IN SHAPING AMERICA'S FUTURE?

WELL, WE ONCE PUT UP A STRUCTURE OF PEACE FOR HENRY KISSINGER.

GREAT.

CAN YOU DO THE JOB, BOYS?

DEPENDS. WHAT KIND OF FOUNDATION ARE YOU FOLKS LOOKING FOR?

$532,

SOMETHING SOLID. SOMETHING WE CAN BUILD ON FOR THE FUTURE.

UH-HUH. HOW MUCH YOU GOT TO SPEND?

000,

ABOUT A HALF A TRILLION DOLLARS.

I'LL DO WHAT I CAN. WHAT DO YOU WANT US TO USE FOR A CORNERSTONE?

000,

UM.. I DUNNO. I GUESS OUR STRATEGIC CAPABILITY.

YOU'RE THE BOSS. COURSE, IF THAT GOES, EVERYTHING ELSE WILL, TOO.

000!

I'LL BE PACKED IN A MINUTE, SPRINGFIELD. JUST MAKE YOURSELF COMFORTABLE.

QUITE A PLACE YOU HAVE HERE, MR. DUKE..

THANKS. I BUILT THIS CABIN MYSELF, BACK IN 1963. DID THE DECORATING AND EVERYTHING.

VERY NICE. MAY I ASK WHY YOU KEEP LAND MINES ON ALL THE SOFAS?

YEAH, I WAS TRYING TO TEACH THE DOGS TO STAY OFF THE FURNITURE.

WHAT DOGS?

OKAY, MR. DUKE, YOU'VE BEEN HERE BEFORE, SO I DON'T HAVE TO TELL YOU THAT THIS CONGRESS IS EVERY BIT AS SPINELESS AS ITS PREDECESSORS!

REMEMBER, THE LEGISLATORS WE DON'T OWN OUTRIGHT ARE SCARED TO DEATH OF MAIL! THEY'RE IN YOUR POCKET, MR. DUKE, SO WHEN YOU WALK THROUGH THAT DOOR, WALK **TALL!**

GOTCHA. I DON'T REALLY HAVE TO READ **ALL** OF THESE CRIME-STOPPER STORIES, DO I?

NO, NO, OF COURSE NOT. YOU JUST BE YOURSELF. YOU'RE OUR ACE IN THE HOLE, MR. DUKE!

I AM? WHAT HAPPENED TO THE WIDOW WHO WASTED NINE MUGGERS?

SHE FOLLOWS YOU. YOU'RE OUR NUMBER-ONE GUN!

"..AND IT IS THE POSITION OF THE NATIONAL RIFLE ASSOCIATION THAT WHEN IT COMES TO ARBITRARY SOCIAL CONTROLS, MORE IS LESS!"

"WHAT IS NEEDED INSTEAD IS A SENSE OF RESTRAINT AND FAIR PLAY. IF OUR ONCE PROUD SCHOOLS WERE TO RESUME THE TEACHING OF.."

EXCUSE ME, MR. DUKE..

I WANT TO GET THIS STRAIGHT. IS IT ACTUALLY YOUR VIEW THAT THE ANSWER TO RISING HAND-GUN VIOLENCE IS A RENEWED EMPHASIS ON SPORTSMANSHIP?

YES?

EXACTLY. WE ADVOCATE A RETURN TO RESPONSIBLE GUNPLAY.

IN OUR ONCE PROUD SCHOOLS?

"THE NATIONAL RIFLE ASSOCIATION THEREFORE OPPOSES ANY AND ALL LEGISLATIVE ATTEMPTS TO CONTROL OUR CONSTITUTIONAL RIGHT TO BEAR ARMS!"

THAT'S THE END OF OUR PREPARED STATEMENT, MR. CHAIRMAN. I'D BE HAPPY TO ENTERTAIN ANY QUESTIONS.

MR. DUKE, DOES YOUR GROUP'S OPPOSITION EXTEND TO A SIMPLE REQUIREMENT OF SERIAL NUMBERS TO AID POLICE IN IDENTIFICATION?

WHAT'S WRONG WITH DENTAL RECORDS?

I WAS REFERRING TO THE GUNS.

SENATOR, THE POINT IS THAT ONCE YOU HAVE GUN CONTROL, THE ONLY PEOPLE LEFT WITH GUNS ARE CRIMINALS!

WHICH WOULD PREVENT A **GREAT** MANY MURDERS, MR. DUKE!

AS YOU WELL KNOW, ALMOST 70% OF ALL MURDERS ARE COMMITTED AMONG FAMILY MEMBERS OR FRIENDS. AND OVER HALF OF THEM INVOLVE HANDGUNS!

EXACTLY! SO LOOK AT IT FROM THE POINT OF VIEW OF THE VICTIM! WHAT IF **YOUR** WIFE WERE ATTACKING YOU WITH A HANDGUN?

I DON'T FOLLOW, MR. DUKE.

WELL, WOULDN'T YOU WANT TO BE IN A POSITION TO RETURN THE FIRE?

WELL, I..UH.. YOU DON'T HAVE TO ANSWER THAT, JIM.

THE QUESTION WE ARE FACING, THEN, MR. DUKE, IS WHETHER THE WISHES OF 80% OF THE AMERICAN PEOPLE WILL AGAIN GO UNHEEDED..

I CANNOT SPEAK FOR MY COLLEAGUES, BUT I FOR ONE AM **FED UP** WITH YOUR DEADLY LOBBY AND ITS FANATICAL DEFENSE OF A TRAGIC AND UNCONSCIONABLE PUBLIC POLICY!

I SEE.

SHALL I PUT YOU DOWN FOR A MILLION POST CARDS, THEN, SENATOR?

DON'T TRY TO INTIMIDATE **ME**, MR. DUKE!

WE'RE BACK TALKING WITH DR. ALI MAHDAVI, '74, ON LEAVE FROM THE IRANIAN REVOLUTIONARY TRIBUNAL, AND HERE ON CAMPUS FOR HIS FIFTH REUNION!

DR. MAHDAVI, FOR OVER A YEAR NOW, AMERICANS HAVE BEEN HEARING ABOUT THE DARK, SINISTER SIDE OF IRAN'S BEARDED HOLY MAN.

I WONDER IF YOU COULD TELL US SOMETHING OF THE OTHER SIDE, THE HUMAN SIDE..

SUCH AS?

WELL, LIKE WHAT DO BEARDED HOLY MEN HAVE FOR BREAKFAST?

SHAHS. IS THIS GOING TO TAKE LONG?

DR. MAHDAVI, HOW DO YOU RESPOND TO CRITICISM THAT YOUR NEW REVOLUTIONARY GOVERNMENT IS RAPIDLY BECOMING THE WORSE OF TWO EVILS?

IT HAS BEEN CHARGED, FOR INSTANCE, THAT THE AYATOLLAH'S ISLAMIC REPUBLIC IS, IN EFFECT, RETURNING IRAN TO THE 14TH CENTURY!

WELL, YES, THAT WAS THE ORIGINAL PLAN, BUT IT IS ENTIRELY POSSIBLE THERE WILL BE SOME COMPROMISE ON THE EXACT ERA.

YOU MEAN, THERE'S A NEW TARGET DATE?

YES, SOME OF US ARE TRYING TO GET IT MOVED UP TO THE AGE OF VOLTAIRE.

I'M SORRY, BUT RICK'S NOT HOME. MAY I ASK WHO'S CALLING?

HALBERSTAM. DAVID HALBERSTAM. I WANT TO INTERVIEW HIM FOR MY NEXT BOOK..

RICK? FOR A BOOK? WHAT SORT OF BOOKS DO YOU WRITE, MR. HALBERSTAM?

I WRITE TOMES. TOMES ABOUT POWER. TOMES LIKE "THE BEST AND THE BRIGHTEST," AND "THE POWERS THAT BE."

THEY'RE MASSIVE BOOKS, BIG, VERY BIG, TOWERING BEST-SELLERS, 750 PAGES, SOMETIMES MORE, THAT'S HOW BIG THEY ARE. THE KIND OF BOOKS ABOUT WHICH MEN LIKE TO SAY, "I OWN THEM."

OH. DO THESE MEN READ THEM?

VERY FEW. ONLY THE BEST.

OH, JUST A MINUTE, MR. HALBERSTAM, HE JUST WALKED IN THE DOOR..

WHO IS IT, BABE?

IT'S DAVID HALBERSTAM. HE WANTS TO INTERVIEW YOU FOR HIS NEW BOOK ON POWER..

MY GOD! WHAT DID YOU TELL HIM?

NOTHING. WHY?

THE MAN'S LIKE A VACUUM CLEANER. NO DETAIL IS TOO SMALL TO SHOW UP IN ONE OF HIS BOOKS.

HELLO?

"HIS VOICE CRACKLED OVER THE LINE, GRUFF, ASSURED..

C'MON, RICK, GO TO SLEEP. IT'S ALMOST TWO..

I CAN'T, JOANIE. I'M JUST TOO NERVOUS ABOUT MY INTERVIEW WITH HALBERSTAM TOMORROW..

NERVOUS? WHAT FOR?

I DUNNO, I GUESS IT'S JUST A LITTLE INTIMIDATING. ALL THE JOURNALISTS HE WRITES ABOUT ARE SO MUCH LARGER THAN LIFE!

THEY'RE ALL SO AWESOME AND BRILLIANT AND WILLFUL, BIG, POWERFUL MEN, ENCRUSTED WITH VIRTUE, EACH KEEPING A "RENDEZVOUS WITH HISTORY"!

MAYBE YOU SHOULD PICK UP SOME BRUT.

RENDEZVOUS WITH HISTORY! I DON'T EVEN OWN AN ENGAGEMENT BOOK!

IT'S AN ENORMOUS PRIVILEGE TO MEET YOU, MR. REDFERN, AN INCREDIBLE, EXTRAORDINARY PRIVILEGE!

THANK YOU, MR. HALBERSTAM. I UNDERSTAND YOU'RE WORKING ON A SEQUEL TO "POWERS THAT BE."

THAT'S RIGHT. I'M CALLING IT "LA CRÈME DE LA CRÈME."

THE BOOK IS ABOUT THE GIANTS OF JOURNALISM, THE BIG, VERY BIG MEN, FORCING LIFE TO EXIST ON THEIR TERMS, THAT'S HOW BIG THEY ARE!

EXIT, JOANIE, STAGE LEFT.

WHERE DO YOU WANT ME?

WHEREVER. SAY, ISN'T THAT THE GREAT SMELL OF BRUT?

HOW DO YOU WANT YOUR COFFEE, MR. HALBERSTAM?

BLACK, JOANIE, VERY BLACK, UTTERLY WITHOUT CREAM AND SUGAR!

AS I TOLD JOANIE ON THE PHONE, I'VE ALWAYS WANTED TO MEET YOU, RICHARD RATHBONE REDFERN. DICK. EVERYONE CALLS YOU DICK, RIGHT?

WHATEVER, YOU'RE AN AWESOME FIGURE ON THE LANDSCAPE, BIG, VERY BIG, ONE OF THE STAGGERING SUCCESS STORIES OF OUR BUSINESS...

NO, RICK.

JOANIE, I THINK YOU SHOULD HEAR THIS.

SHE ALREADY KNOWS. HER INTUITION IS EXTRAORDINARY, ALMOST GOD-LIKE.

YOU KNOW, DICK, WHEN I THINK OF YOUR NEW YORK GLORY DAYS BACK ON THE OLD "TRIBUNE," IT JUST SENDS CHILLS UP MY SPINE.

THOSE WERE THE DAYS, ALL RIGHT.

WERE THEY EVER! I DON'T THINK I'LL EVER FORGET YOUR COLUMNS, HOW YOU USED TO FILL THEM WITH ANECDOTES..

THEY WERE BIG, GLISTENING ANECDOTES, VERY MOVING, VERY BRIGHT, ANECDOTES THAT PILED ONE UPON ANOTHER TO FORM A SPRAWLING MOSAIC OF OUR TIMES, THAT WAS HOW BRILLIANT THEY WERE.

OF COURSE, I WAS ONLY STAMPS EDITOR THEN.

NO MATTER. YOU OWNED THE TOWN.

OKAY, THAT BRINGS US UP TO THE LONG, HOT SUMMER OF '68. THAT'S WHEN YOU WERE SENT TO WASHINGTON TO COVER RESURRECTION CITY, RIGHT?

UM.. YEAH, THAT'S RIGHT..

AND IT WAS THERE THAT YOU BECAME SOMETHING OF A DEITY TO YOUR COLLEAGUES, THEY WERE IN AWE OF YOU, BUT THAT DID NOT LESSEN YOUR DEDICATION, IT INCREASED IT, RIGHT?

I JUST DIDN'T KNOW ANY OTHER WAY, DAVID.

OF COURSE, YOU DIDN'T. GOD, YOU LOVED YOUR WORK!

DAVID, BEFORE WE GO ON, I GOTTA ASK YOU-DO YOU REALLY BELIEVE IN THIS JOURNALIST-AS-STAR NONSENSE?

GOD, NO! IT'S THE WORST THING THAT CAN HAPPEN TO BOTH JOURNALISM AND THE PUBLIC!

BUT YOUR BOOKS ARE A MONUMENT TO JUST THAT ADULATION!

MAYBE. DEBATABLE. SUBJECT TO DEBATE. BUT I THINK I SEE YOUR POINT..

WHAT YOU'RE SAYING IS THAT THE CELEBRATION OF THE JOURNALIST IS CORRUPTING, THAT WHEN HE BECOMES BIGGER, MUCH BIGGER, THAN HIS STORY, IT DOES NOT HEIGHTEN HIS EFFECTIVENESS, IT DIMINISHES IT, RIGHT?

EXACTLY. TAKE WOODWARD AND BERNSTEIN..

GODS. I KISS THEIR GUCCIS.

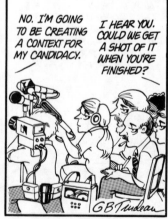

GOVERNOR, COULD YOU TELL US A LITTLE ABOUT WHAT YOU BELIEVE IN?

MY BELIEFS AND CONVICTIONS ARE WHAT THE PEOPLE CHOOSE TO PROJECT ON ME. I SEE NO NEED FOR ANY OF MY OWN.

BUT WITHOUT CONVICTIONS, HOW CAN YOU ADDRESS SOCIAL NEEDS?

THERE'S NO SUCH THING AS SOCIAL NEEDS, THERE ARE ONLY POLITICAL PRESSURES. I PROMISE TO RESPOND TO ALL OF THEM.

THE PROBLEM IS THIS: WE HAVE A LEADERSHIP CRISIS IN THE CONTROL TOWER OF SPACESHIP AMERICA. THE PEOPLE WANT A LEADER. A LEADER TODAY IS SOMEONE WHO WILL REPRESENT THEIR EVERY WHIM.

I THOUGHT THAT WAS A FOLLOWER.

THE LAST SHALL BE FIRST. THE FIRST SHALL TAKE NEW HAMPSHIRE.

YES, YOU..

GOVERNOR, FOR SYMBOLIC PURPOSES, YOU HAVE GONE TO SOME PAINS TO KEEP YOUR PRIVATE LIFE IN THE PUBLIC EYE..

VIRTUALLY NOBODY HASN'T HEARD THAT YOU DRIVE AN OLD PLYMOUTH, LIVE IN A SMALL APARTMENT, LIKE MEXICAN FOOD, BUDDHISM, BOB DYLAN, ETC., ETC.

MY QUESTION, GOVERNOR, IS HOW FAR ARE YOU WILLING TO GO IN TRANSFORMING YOUR PRIVATE LIFE INTO NOTHING BUT AN ONGOING PRESS RELEASE?

YOU WANT TO HANDLE THAT ONE, LINDA?

OH, WOW.. NO.

GOVERNOR BROWN, IF I MAY JUST FOLLOW UP ON THAT QUESTION ABOUT YOUR BOX OFFICE PRIORITIES..

WOULD YOU SAY THAT EVEN THE FUTURE OF YOUR RELATIONSHIP WITH MS. RONSTADT IS RESPONSIVE TO PUBLIC MOOD?

YES, OF COURSE. WHY GET MARRIED WHEN A RECENT POLL SHOWS THAT 90% OF CALIFORNIAN VOTERS COULD CARE LESS IF LINDA AND I GOT MARRIED OR NOT?

I'VE GOT A NEW ALBUM COMING OUT, THOUGH.

YES, IT ALL COULD CHANGE.

GOVERNOR, ARE YOU COMMITTED TO ANYTHING BEYOND THE PUBLIC MOOD? FOR INSTANCE, YOU NOW SUPPORT A BALANCED BUDGET, BUT LESS THAN A YEAR AGO, YOU BITTERLY OPPOSED PROP 13!

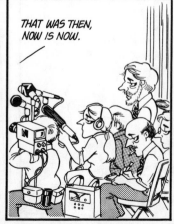

THAT WAS THEN, NOW IS NOW.

UH.. EXCUSE ME, SIR, BUT I'M FROM WASHINGTON. I DON'T KNOW ABOUT CALIFORNIA, BUT BACK EAST THAT WOULD BE A FATUOUS AND CYNICAL ANSWER. I WONDER IF YOU COULD DO BETTER.

EAST IS EAST, WEST IS WEST.

THANK YOU.

DELACOURT'S *RESIGNING?* ARE YOU SURE ABOUT THIS, RED-FERN?

POSITIVE, BOSS. HE'LL ANNOUNCE TOMORROW! I ONLY HELD OFF THIS LONG AS A PERSONAL FAVOR.

BUT WHY FOR JERRY BROWN? IT DOESN'T MAKE ANY SENSE!

IT DOES IF YOU'RE IN THE SYMBOL BIZ. BROWN'S WHOLE CAREER IS ONE SUSTAINED METAPHOR.

WAS DELA-COURT BEHIND THE GOVERNOR'S SURFIN'SAFARI LAST MONTH?

I DOUBT IT. HE WAS BUSY ORCHESTRATING CARTER'S RADIATION BOOTIES AROUND THAT TIME..

FROM PAP TO POP. I DON'T GET IT.

BESIDES, DUANE'S A MORALIST. HE WOULD HAVE GONE WITH SEPARATE TENTS.

ton Pos

DAY, MAY 8, 1979   15

Californian Creates 'Context' For White House Bid

Vows Commitment To Public Mood

By Rick Redfern
SACRAMENTO,
California, May 7 —
oday, in a press
ference at t
rni

THE WAS

Carter Symbol Chief to Defect

Cardigans Seen in Sacramento

By Rick Redfe

Secretary of Symbolism Duane Delacourt
5-8   THE CAPITOL

WASHINGTON
May 7 — The
Phonathon,
Tree House
Fireside C
said he w
for

Campaign '80:   THE WAS

Brown Assembles 'Mellow Mafia'

Tom Hayden, Others, to Sell Out

Analysis by Rick Redfern

Governor Jerry Brown is
sometimes compared to a
Rorschach test; people
see in him what they
want. How else
to explain
th

B
uz
wor
buzz
words
buzz w
rds buzz
words

MY, HAVEN'T WE BEEN A BUSY BOY!

WE NEED THE MONEY.

JOANIE, WHAT WOULD YOU SAY TO HAVING A SMALL DINNER FOR DUANE BEFORE HE LEAVES FOR SACRAMENTO?

THAT'S A FINE IDEA, RICK! WE COULD ASK A FEW OF HIS COLLEAGUES FROM THE DEPARTMENT OF SYMBOLISM!

MAYBE HAVE SORT OF A THEME PARTY..

WELL, SURE! WE COULD ALL WEAR JEANS AND CARDIGANS!

WELL, I DON'T KNOW ABOUT THAT. BELIEVE IT OR NOT, DUANE LIKES TO UNWIND IN A THREE-PIECE SUIT!

DUANE? BUT HE'S WORN JEANS TO THE WHITE HOUSE FOR THREE YEARS!

INCREDIBLE, HUH? HE SAYS HE FELT LIKE A BUM, BUT IT WAS HIS JOB.

SHEILA? HI, IT'S RICK..

HI, RICK! HOW'S IT GOING?

JUST FINE, SHEILA. IS DUANE HOME?

SURE, HOLD ON, I'LL GET HIM. HE'S IN THE BATHROOM PRACTICING FOR CALIFORNIA.

"PRACTICING"?

HAVE A NICE DAY. HAVE A NICE DAY. HAVE A NICE DAY..

DUANE?

HEY, RICK! WHAT'S HAP-PENING, MAN?

WELL, JOANIE AND I WERE WONDERING IF YOU COULD MAKE IT OVER TOMOR-ROW NIGHT FOR A LITTLE FARE-WELL PARTY..

HEY, SOUNDS LIKE A GREAT DYNAMIC! IN-TERACTIONWISE, I CAN GET BEHIND IT!

HELLO? DUANE? IS THAT YOU?

SURE! I'M JUST PRACTICING MY CALIFORNIAN. WHAT'S YOUR TIME CONTEXT? CAN YOU RELATE TO EIGHT?

UH.. I CAN GIVE IT MY BEST SHOT.

GREAT! HAVE A NICE DAY. SAVE THE WHALES.

HEY, DID YOU GET HOLD OF DUANE, RICK? CAN HE COME TOMORROW?

I'M NOT SURE. I COULDN'T UNDERSTAND HIM.

WHAT DO YOU MEAN?

HE KEPT SPEAKING CALIFORNIAN TO ME. I THINK HE'S BEEN STUDYING IT!

THAT'S RIGHT, HE HAS! SHEILA TOLD ME HE'S TAKING CORRESPON-DENCE COURSES FROM THE CALIFORNIA INSTI-TUTE FOR THE MELLOW!

WELL, HE'S VERY PRO-FICIENT. I COULDN'T MAKE OUT A WORD HE SAID.

OH, C'MON, RICHARD, YOU GO OUT TO CALIFORNIA ALL THE TIME!

YEAH, BUT I ALWAYS END UP HAVING TO POINT AT THE MENUS.

JOANIE, SHEILA AND I ARE REALLY BLOWN AWAY BY YOU FOLKS DOING DINNER FOR US!

NOT AT ALL, DUANE. WE'RE HAPPY YOU COULD COME.

HUH?

WELL, IT'S REALLY A GREAT CON-TEXT FOR SHARING ENERGY!

THAT'S "MELLOW-SPEAK," JOANIE. WE'VE BEEN STUDYING DR. DAN ASHER'S NEW BOOK!

FOR SURE!

WE'RE TRYING TO LEARN CALIFORNIAN BEFORE WE MAKE THE BIG MOVE!

YOU'RE FLASHING ON MY CHEST HAIRS, AREN'T YOU, JOANIE?

UM..

THAT'S OKAY, JOANIE. YOU CAN BE UPFRONT ABOUT IT.

HI, THERE, BUDDY!

WELL, WELL, THE GUEST OF HONOR! EXPECTING A DULL PARTY?

HOW'S THAT?

THE BOOK. YOU BROUGHT A BOOK.

OH, YOU MEAN MY COPY OF "MELLOW-SPEAK"! I'M FLASHING ON CAL-IFORNIAN, RICK, TAK-ING RESPONSIBILITY FOR MY NEW SPACE!

I SEE. HOW ABOUT RUN-NING THAT BY ME IN WASHINGTON-IAN?

I'M IMPACTING MY OPTIONS.

WELL, WHY DIDN'T YOU SAY SO?

SOLDIERS OF MISFORTUNE

Q: Given the uncertainties of the long hostage crisis, wasn't writing about it fairly risky?

A: That's putting it mildly. The day after I finished the series on Reverend Sloan's visit to Teheran, the Desert One debacle broke. I had to kill the whole series, rewrite it, and submit it again after passions over the episode subsided. Strangely enough — considering some of the things I was writing about the students — a number of the strips got through to the hostages.[1] The Iranians had reached a conclusion very familiar to me: that there is no danger of finding anything of substance in the comics.

[1]On January 15, 1980, hostage William F. Keough, Jr., wrote home that "spirits of Americans can be lifted in many ways; thus, to my delight, Trudeau got the message through that the U.S. is very much aware of its citizens, now in their tenth week of imprisonment."

HI, BOSS. WHAT'S UP?

RICK, I WANT YOU TO GET OVER TO THE HILL TODAY AND COVER THE LINKAGE HEARINGS.

WHAT LINKAGE HEARINGS?

YOU KNOW, JACKSON, CHURCH AND COMPANY. THEY'VE JUST FORMED A NEW TASK FORCE TO LINK SALT WITH A SOVIET PRESENCE IN CUBA.

IT'S ALL VERY NOSTALGIC. THEY'VE EVEN NAMED IT AFTER KISSINGER'S OLD CODE NAME FOR THE MAYAGUEZ RESCUE.

GOOD MORNING, OPERATION MANHOOD, MAY I HELP YOU?

GBTrudeau

GOOD EVENING. TODAY "OPERATION MANHOOD" WENT INTO HIGH GEAR AS SENATORS CHURCH, JACKSON AND BAKER FORMALLY OPENED THEIR SPECIAL LINKAGE HEARINGS.

WAVING A PARCHMENT COPY OF THE MONROE DOCTRINE ABOVE HIS HEAD, JACKSON DEMANDED THAT THE PRESIDENT FACE DOWN THE SOVIETS "EYEBALL TO EYEBALL, LIKE A REAL MAN."

IN ANOTHER DEVELOPMENT, THE SENATORS ALSO PLEDGED TO INVESTIGATE NEW EVIDENCE LINKING RUSSIAN SABOTEURS WITH THE SINKING OF THE "MAINE."

FROM THE CHEAP SEATS ON CAPITOL HILL, THIS IS ROLAND HEDLEY, JR.

GBTrudeau

GENERAL, LET'S GET RIGHT DOWN TO BRASS TACKS! IS THE SOVIET UNION TURNING CUBA INTO A FORTRESS-STATE?

WELL, THE EVIDENCE CERTAINLY SUGGESTS SO, SENATOR JACKSON.

FOR INSTANCE, A RECENT SR-71 FLIGHT BROUGHT BACK SOME AERIAL PHOTOGRAPHS OF A CUBAN MILITARY SUPPLY DEPOT. ONE OF THE PHOTOGRAPHS REVEALED A SOVIET COMMISSARY OFFICER EXAMINING A REQUISITION FORM...

WHEN TRANSLATED FROM THE ORIGINAL SPANISH, THE FORM WAS FOUND TO CONTAIN A REQUEST FOR NEARLY 1,500 CZECH STAPLE GUNS.

STAPLE GUNS? WITH AN OFFENSIVE CAPABILITY?

LET'S JUST SAY THE TECHNOLOGY IS AVAILABLE.

GENERAL, IN YOUR OPINION, DOES THE PRESENCE OF THE SOVIET BRIGADE PRESENT A LEGITIMATE THREAT TO THE SECURITY OF THIS COUNTRY?

SENATOR BAKER, I'D BE LESS THAN CANDID IF I DENIED IT.

MY PERSONAL EVALUATION IS THAT THESE 3,000 RUSSIAN SHOCK TROOPS COULD BE EASILY DEPLOYED TO SPEARHEAD A MASSIVE AMPHIBIOUS ASSAULT AGAINST THE COASTLINES OF FLORIDA, ALABAMA AND SOME PARTS OF MISSISSIPPI.

HAVING ESTABLISHED THESE BEACHHEADS, THE SOVIETS WOULD THEN BE FREE TO FAN OUT ACROSS THE SOUTH, DISRUPTING TRAFFIC, AND EFFECTIVELY CRIPPLING THE TOURIST INDUSTRY SO VITAL TO THE ECONOMY OF THE REGION.

MY GOD! THINK OF THE JOBS!

YES, SIR. AND THAT'S ONLY ONE SCENARIO.

GBTrudeau

SENATOR CHURCH, IF I MAY JUST MAKE ONE LAST COMMENT..

OF COURSE, GENERAL.

SENATOR, I THINK IT'S FAIR TO SAY THAT IF IT HAD NOT BEEN FOR THE VIGILANCE OF THE U.S. SENATE, THIS MAJOR CRISIS IN CUBA MIGHT HAVE DEGENERATED INTO A MINOR DIPLOMATIC SQUABBLE EASILY HANDLED BY THE STATE DEPARTMENT.

BY REFUSING TO FAN THE FLAMES OF MODERATION, A CALM, NEGOTIATED SOLUTION HAS BEEN NARROWLY AVERTED. THANKS TO YOU AND "OPERATION MANHOOD," THE AMERICAN PEOPLE HAVE BEEN GIVEN ANOTHER CHANCE TO SHOW THAT THEY'RE STILL NUMBER ONE!

THANK YOU, GENERAL, I APPRECIATE THAT.

THANK YOU, SENATOR. AND GOOD LUCK WITH YOUR RE-ELECTION.

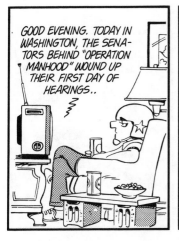

GOOD EVENING. TODAY IN WASHINGTON, THE SENATORS BEHIND "OPERATION MANHOOD" WOUND UP THEIR FIRST DAY OF HEARINGS..

AFTER ONLY TWO HOURS OF TESTIMONY, PANEL MEMBERS CAME SURPRISINGLY CLOSE TO AGREEING ON THE HARD-LINE LINKAGE PACKAGE THEY EXPECT TO SEND TO THE WHITE HOUSE.

ONLY LAST-MINUTE PANGS OF CONSCIENCE PREVENTED SENATOR CHURCH FROM ENDORSING SENATOR DOLE'S RESOLUTION CALLING ON THE PRESIDENT TO "LEAD THE COUNTRY TO THE BRINK OF NUCLEAR CONFRONTATION."

THE RESOLUTION WAS SENT BACK TO COMMITTEE FOR REWORDING.

HEY, MIKE! DID YOU KNOW "PLAYBOY" WAS DOING A PICTORIAL ON "THE GIRLS OF THE IVY LEAGUE"?

YEAH, I HEARD. THEIR PHOTOGRAPHER'S ARRIVING ON CAMPUS THIS WEEK.

"$100 FOR FULLY CLOTHED, $200 FOR SEMI-NUDE OR DORSAL, $400 FOR FULL FRONTAL"..

THE GUY'S WASTING HIS TIME IF YOU ASK ME.

HEY, C'MON, MIKE, THAT'S A PRETTY GOOD PIECE OF CHANGE!

SURE, BUT SHOW ME A SINGLE WOMAN ON THIS CAMPUS WHO'D TURN SEX OBJECT FOR ANY AMOUNT OF MONEY!

HEY, BOOPSIE!

BUT, OF COURSE. YOUR OWN GIRL FRIEND.

YOU WANT ME TO POSE FOR "PLAYBOY", B.D.?

WHY NOT? YOU'VE GOT THE BOD FOR IT! BESIDES, IT'S AN EASY 400 BUCKS!

GEE, I DUNNO, B.D..

LOOK, I'M TELLING YOU, BOOPSIE, IT'S A HELL OF AN OPPORTUNITY! IF YOUR PICTURE MAKES IT, YOU'LL BE FAMOUS!

ME? FAMOUS?

WELL, SURE! WHY, THAT MAG IS SCOPED EVERY MONTH BY MILLIONS OF GUYS!

GEE.. I WOULD LIKE TO BREAK INTO SHOW BUSINESS..

EXACTLY! AND THIS SURE AS HELL BEATS DRAMA SCHOOL!

..AND TELL THOSE CLOWNS UP IN SACRAMENTO THAT JERRY'S **SERIOUS** ABOUT HIS PLANETARIUM APPROPRIATIONS BILL!

OKAY, I HEAR YOU.

ALSO, SEE THAT THE DRIVER PICKS UP THE GOVERNOR AT 6:30 TO TAKE HIM TO THE ANTI-NUKE CLAM BAKE.

GOT IT. ANYTHING ELSE?

YES. DO YOU KNOW IF SKYLAB HAS LANDED YET?

NOT SURE. WHY?

JERRY WOULD LIKE TO BE THERE TO MEET IT.

OKAY. I'LL PUT OUT SOME FEELERS.

SYMBOLS. DELACOURT HERE.

HI, DUANE, IT'S GRAY. WE'VE GOT A PROBLEM.

NBC HAS BROKEN A STORY THAT'S GIVING US SOME P.R. HEADACHES. THEY'RE CLAIMING THAT JERRY ONCE SOLICITED A $1000 CONTRIBUTION FROM A LOCAL MAFIA BIGGIE.

WELL?

WELL, WHAT?

IS IT TRUE?

THAT'S NOT YOUR DEPARTMENT! I MEAN, OF **COURSE** NOT!

LET ME GET THIS STRAIGHT, GRAY— **WHO** EXACTLY DID JERRY SOLICIT THE CONTRIBUTION FROM?

A GUY NAMED SIDNEY KORSHAK. HE'S THE LOCAL LOW-LIFE, AN ALUMNUS FROM THE CAPONE MOB..

UNFORTUNATELY, IT DOESN'T STOP WITH THE CONTRIBUTION. JERRY ALSO TRIED TO CLOSE A RACE TRACK AS A FAVOR TO A STRIKING UNION. GUESS WHO WAS REPRESENTING THE UNION?

COULD BE A COINCIDENCE, RIGHT?

WELL, THAT'S UP TO YOU, DUANE. JERRY WANTS YOU TO WORK UP A P.R. STRATEGY AND MEET HIM AT EL ADOBE FOR DINNER.

GRAY, I DON'T "WORK UP P.R. STRATEGIES." I CREATE SYMBOLS.

SUIT YOURSELF. BUT HE'S GOING TO WANT TO SEE SOME LAYOUTS.

GRAY TELLS ME WE'VE GOT A BIT OF A PROBLEM, GOVERNOR.

YEAH, AND IT'S NOT FAIR. I DON'T EVEN **KNOW** THIS CREEP KORSHAK!

YOU DON'T?

OKAY, SO I MAY HAVE RUN INTO HIM A FEW TIMES AT LEW WASSERMAN'S PARTIES.

WHO?

LEW WASSERMAN. HE'S A MOVIE MOGUL. HE HAS TO DEAL WITH KORSHAK TO GET HIS MOVIES MADE.

MOVIES? GOVERNOR, WHAT'S THAT GOT TO DO WITH..

LOOK, THAT'S ALL I KNOW. I WAS IN AFRICA. I'VE GOT WITNESSES.

GOVERNOR, IF I'M GO-ING TO HANDLE THE PRESS ON THIS ONE, I'M GOING TO NEED ALL THE INFORMATION YOU CAN GIVE ME.

NO PROBLEM. I HAVE NOTHING TO HIDE.

GOOD. NOW, WHEN THE NBC REPORTER ASKED YOU WHY YOU SOLICITED $1000 FROM A KNOWN ORGANIZED CRIME FIGURE, HOW EX-ACTLY DID YOU JUSTIFY IT?

I POINTED OUT THAT EVEN JANE FONDA HAD ONCE BEEN INVESTIGAT-ED BY THE F.B.I.

WHICH IS WHY YOU APPOINTED HER TO YOUR ARTS COMMIS-SION?

ABSOLUTELY. I BELIEVE THESE PEOPLE CAN BE REHABILITATED.

SO WHAT THEY'RE SAYING IS THAT I TRIED TO CLOSE A HORSE RACING TRACK AT THE BIDDING OF AN UNDISPUTED MOBSTER! ME, A FORMER JESUIT, FOR GOD'S SAKE!

IS IT TRUE, BOSS?

IS WHAT TRUE?

IS IT TRUE THE FIX WAS IN?

THEY MAKE A PRETTY FAIR TACO HERE, DON'T YOU THINK?

BOSS..

WHAT'S "AN UN-DISPUTED MOBSTER" REALLY MEAN, ANYWAY? ISN'T THAT JUST A TIRED CLICHÉ?

DUANE, THE BOSS IS REAL-LY STARTING TO FEEL THE HEAT, BUDDY,

I'M ON IT, GRAY. I CALLED A PRESS CONFERENCE FOR THIS AFTERNOON.

HOW ARE YOU PLANNING TO EXPLAIN JER-RY'S ASSOCI-ATION WITH KORSHAK?

WELL, I THOUGHT I'D SAY THAT BROWN IS INTRIGUED BY THE MAFIA ONLY AS A SOURCE OF IDEAS.

I'LL POINT OUT THAT ORGANIZED CRIME IS ONE OF THE FEW LABOR-INTENSIVE INDUSTRIES TO BE BOTH SELF-REGULATORY AND COST-EFFICIENT.

SO WE ALL HAVE MUCH TO LEARN, ETC.?

EXACTLY. I THOUGHT I'D SHOW SOME FLOW CHARTS.

UH.. ROLAND, IF YOU DON'T MIND, I'D LIKE TO GET THIS THING STARTED..

JUST ONE QUICK STAND-UP, BUDDY, AND WE'LL BE OUT OF YOUR WAY!

THIS IS ROLAND HEDLEY, JR., IN LOS ANGELES. TONIGHT, ABC NEWS LOOKS AT A SORDID STORY ABOUT THE TANGLED DESTINIES OF A GOVERNOR, A RACKETEER, AND A MOVIE TYCOON!

IT'S ALSO A STORY OF INFLUENCE AND FIXING, BUT HEY, LET'S LET THE GRAND JURY SORT THAT OUT! FOR NOW, LET'S LISTEN TO BROWN SPOKESMAN DUANE DELACOURT TRY TO DEFEND HIS BOSS!

UH..

THIRTY SECONDS, BUDDY.

ROLLING!

LADIES AND GENTLEMEN, FOR YOUR GUIDANCE, I'VE PREPARED THE FOLLOWING STATEMENT: "APART FROM A $1000 CONTRIBUTION, GOVERNOR BROWN HAS HAD **NO** ASSOCIATION WITH REPUTED GANGSTER SIDNEY KORSHAK."

EXCUSE ME, DUANE. IN 1974, THE RESTAURANT EMPLOYEES UNION GAVE BROWN OVER $50,000. KORSHAK'S CONNECTIONS WITH THE UNION ARE WELL-KNOWN.

OH..

YOU WANT ME TO FIX THAT ON YOUR COPIES?

NO, NO, WE CAN REMEMBER.

DUANE, HOW FAR BACK DOES JERRY GO WITH SIDNEY KORSHAK?

I ALREADY TOLD YOU! THEY BARELY KNOW EACH OTHER!

DID JERRY KNOW HIM WHEN HE WAS RUNNING WITH JAKE "GREASY THUMB" GUZIK, AL CAPONE'S OLD ACCOUNTANT?

"GREASY THUMB" GUZIK?

LADIES AND GENTLEMEN, BEFORE THIS GETS OUT OF CONTROL, MAY I JUST REMIND YOU THAT WE'RE TALKING ABOUT THE **GOVERNOR** OF THE STATE OF **CALIFORNIA!**

DUANE, DOES JERRY PACK A PIECE?

I DOUBT IT. HE'S PARTIAL TO SOFTWARE.

DUANE, SIDNEY KORSHAK HAS BEEN CHARACTERIZED BY THE JUSTICE DEPARTMENT AS ONE OF THE MOST POWERFUL UNDERWORLD FIGURES IN THE COUNTRY.

AND YET JERRY BROWN PARTIES WITH HIM, AND MOVIE MOGULS LIKE MCA'S LEW WASSERMAN AND PARAMOUNT'S ROBERT EVANS ARE CLOSE, PERSONAL FRIENDS OF HIS.

EVEN JERRY'S FATHER, PAT BROWN, LUNCHES WITH HIM REGULARLY. DUANE, COULD YOU EXPLAIN SIDNEY KORSHAK'S MAGIC?

HIS MAGIC EMERGES. HE VIEWS THE STATUTE OF LIMITATIONS AS A PROCESS.

I'LL BET.

FOR THE **LAST** TIME, GOVERNOR BROWN HAS **NEVER..**

THAT WAS THE VOICE OF PROTEST FROM THE BROWN CAMP HERE TODAY!

TOP FLACK DUANE DELACOURT PROVED ADAMANT IN HIS DENIAL OF ANY BROWN WRONGDOING IN A SCHEME TO HELP RACKETEER SIDNEY KORSHAK'S RACE TRACK UNION!

BUT ABC NEWS HAS LEARNED THAT BROWN WAS SEEN LUNCHING AT "THE BISTRO," KORSHAK'S RESTAURANT, THE SAME DAY HE MOVED TO CLOSE THE TRACK!

NOW, WAIT JUST A **MINUTE,** ROLAND..

BROWN WAS SAID TO HAVE HAD THE DUCK.

"..AND OF THE LAST 112 DAYS, BROWN HAS BEEN IN SACRAMENTO FOR ONLY THREE."

I THOUGHT THINGS WERE A LITTLE QUIET AROUND HERE..

"MOREOVER, GOVERNOR BROWN HAS AN IMAGE PROBLEM. DESPITE THE REASSURANCES OF CONVERTED PUNDITS, HE IS STILL WIDELY PERCEIVED AS FLAKY."

"FLAKY"! RICK, I CAN'T BELIEVE A WRITER OF YOUR STATURE IS STILL PUSHING THAT TIRED CLAPTRAP! JUST BECAUSE A MAN HAS A FEW EXOTIC INTERESTS DOESN'T MAKE HIM A FLAKE!

I COULDN'T AGREE MORE, DUANE, BUT YOU'RE MISSING THE POINT. THE ZEN AND THE WHALES AND THE ROCK STAR GIRL FRIEND HAVE NOTHING TO DO WITH WHY PEOPLE THINK HE'S A FLAKE..

PEOPLE THINK HE'S FLAKY BECAUSE HE IS A MAN WITH A MILLION IDEAS AND A GENUINE COMMITMENT TO NONE; BECAUSE OF HIS PASSION FOR PREVAILING WINDS; BECAUSE HE HAS THE ATTENTION SPAN OF A FIVE-YEAR-OLD.

HE'S TOYING WITH US, DUANE. HE'S A MAN WHO TAKES POSITIONS NOT BECAUSE HE BELIEVES IN THEM, BUT BECAUSE SOMEONE TOLD HIM HE HAD TO HAVE A FEW TO RUN FOR PRESIDENT!

BUT THAT'S NOT FLAKY, DAMMIT, THAT'S CYNICAL!

I'M NOT GOING TO QUIBBLE WITH YOU, DUANE.

DUKE! HOLD YOUR FIRE! I'M A FRIEND!

I'LL BE THE JUDGE OF THAT, STRANGER! PUT YOUR HANDS UP WHERE I CAN SEE 'EM!

DUKE, IT'S ME! YOUR OL' BUSINESS ASSOCIATE FROM SAMOA— JIM ANDREWS!

ANDREWS? YOU MEAN, UNIVERSAL *PETROLEUM* ANDREWS?

THEN YOU HAVEN'T FORGOTTEN!

FORGOTTEN? HOW DOES ONE FORGET A GUTLESS, GOUGING OIL PUSHER WHO'D TRADE HIS OWN GRANDMOTHER TO THE ARABS!

HEY, C'MON, AT LEAST HER SINUSES CLEARED UP..

STILL BANKING AT GENEVA SAVINGS AND LOAN, ARE YOU?

SO, DUKE! HOW'S TRICKS?

HOW'S "TRICKS"?

ANDREWS, A MAN CAPABLE OF CREATING A MASSIVE OIL SHORTAGE BY MAKING A SINGLE PHONE CALL DOES NOT FLY HALFWAY ACROSS THE COUNTRY TO ASK ABOUT "TRICKS"!

QUITE RIGHT. I'LL BE DIRECT: WHAT'S YOUR GOING RATE FOR COMMITTING AN UNSPEAKABLY DEPRAVED BUT HIGHLY PATRIOTIC ACT?

$100,000, PLUS 10% OF THE GROSS.

I RESPECT YOU TOO MUCH TO HAGGLE.

BUT I DON'T WORK WITH ALBANIANS! AND CHILDREN AND PETS ARE EXTRA.

ONLY ONE THING MISSING FROM THIS CONTRACT, ANDREWS: ANY MENTION OF THE JOB!

ALL IN GOOD TIME, DUKE. THE STAKES ARE HIGH IN THIS BUSINESS. I'M SURE YOU APPRECIATE THE NEED FOR SECURITY.

YEAH, ESPECIALLY MY OWN! YOU'LL HAVE TO DO BETTER THAN THAT, ANDREWS!

I ASSURE YOU, DUKE, YOUR MISSION FOR THE COMPANY IS QUITE WITHIN THE SCOPE OF YOUR CONSIDERABLE TALENTS.

DAMMIT, MAN! I HAVE TO KNOW WHAT I'M GETTING INTO!

DUKE, LET'S JUST SAY THAT IF YOU SUCCEED, YOU MAY WELL ALTER THE ENTIRE COURSE OF AMERICAN ECONOMIC HISTORY!

ME? THE COURSE OF HISTORY? HOW LONG WOULD THAT TAKE?

TWO WEEKS, TOPS. AND WE HANDLE ALL THE PAPERWORK.

DUKE, MAY I JUST SAY ON BEHALF OF THE BOARD OF UNIVERSAL PETROLEUM HOW GLAD WE ARE TO HAVE YOU ABOARD!

TELL ME, ANDREWS, DO YOU EVER TIRE OF PLAYING GOD?

ON OCCASION. SOMETIMES IT CAN BE AN AWESOME RESPONSIBILITY. REMEMBER THE 1974 RECESSION?

YEAH?

I CAUSED IT.

YOU *WHAT?*

I JUST GOT BEHIND IN MY MAIL. PURE CARELESSNESS.

YOU KNOW, I *THOUGHT* THAT HAD YOUR FINGERPRINTS ON IT!

SORRY, "MOTHER," NO WORD FROM "EAGLE" YET.

DAMN! THERE'S GOING TO BE HELL TO PAY AT THE NEXT BOARD MEETING FOR THIS!

IF THEY'VE GOT "EAGLE," WE'VE LOST "DIPSTICK," COMPROMISED OUR LIBYAN SPOT MARKET OPERATIVES, AND PROBABLY EXPOSED THE KUWAIT PAYOFFS! WE'RE STARING AT A MILLION BARREL SHORT-FALL!

OH.

WHATEVER HAPPENED TO EXPLORATORY DRILLING?

TOO RISKY. YOU DON'T SUPPOSE "EAGLE" WAS TOO STONED TO PULL HIS CORD, DO YOU?

"MOTHER"! A CABLE FROM TEHERAN!

FINALLY! GIVE IT HERE!

"REGRET TO IN-FORM YOU EAGLE HAS BOMBED. DIPSTICK."

MOTHER OF ALLAH! THEY CAUGHT HIM ALREADY?

GOD HELP US ALL.

A TOURIST? WITH OVER $200,000 IN CASH?

SO I'M NOT KARL MALDEN. SUE ME.

MR. McMEEL? ANDREWS HERE. I'M AFRAID I HAVE BAD NEWS, SIR. "EAGLE" HAS BOMBED.

DAMN! YOU SURE?

YES, SIR. IF HE TALKS, IT COULD BE EMBARRASS-ING FOR THE COMPANY! THE WORD IS HE'LL BE TRIED AND EXECUTED IN THE MORNING.

MY GOD.. THAT'S TERRIBLE..

YES, SIR. HE WAS A GOOD FRIEND.

YOU GOT SOMEONE ELSE LINED UP?

YEAH, BUT I THINK WE OUGHTA WAIT A DECENT INTERVAL. AT LEAST UNTIL THE STOCK MAR-KET CLOSES.

GOOD EVENING. TODAY FORMER UNITED STATES AMBASSADOR DUKE WAS CAPTURED WHILE PARA-CHUTING INTO THE AHVAZ OIL FIELDS IN IRAN. ROLAND HEDLEY HAS DETAILS.

THE REVOLUTIONARY GOVERNMENT OF THE AYATOLLAH KHOMEINI ANNOUNCED TONIGHT THAT THE ONETIME WASHINGTON REDSKINS FIELD GENERAL WOULD BE TRIED AND CONVICTED OF HIGH CRIMES AGAINST GOD.

ALTHOUGH DUE PROCESS AS PRACTICED IN THE WEST IS VIRTUALLY UNKNOWN HERE, ABC NEWS HAS LEARNED THAT AMBASSA-DOR DUKE WAS PERMITTED THE CUSTOMARY PHONE CALL..

HEY, MAN, THOSE ARE THE BREAKS.

DAMMIT, BRENNER! I NEED THOSE KRUGERRANDS!

THIS IS ROLAND HEDLEY. IT'S A BLEAK, DARK MORNING HERE IN TEHERAN AS THE ESPIONAGE TRIAL OF FORMER AMBASSADOR DUKE GETS UNDER WAY!

IN THE NEW IRAN, THE ISLAMIC KANGAROO COURTS ARE CUSTOMARILY GAVELED TO ORDER AT AN UNGODLY 4:00 A.M.! TODAY SHOULD BE NO EXCEPTION.

TENSION HAS BEEN MOUNTING HERE ALL WEEK AS..

THE WHOLE WORLD IS *WATCHING*! THE WHOLE WORLD IS *WATCHING*!

AH, HERE COMES THE DEFENDANT NOW!

THE WHOLE.. >THUD!< & UNH!

GBTrudeau

THE REVOLUTIONARY TRIBUNAL WILL NOW COME TO ORDER! THE COURT WILL HEAR THE ISLAMIC REPUBLIC OF IRAN VS. AMBASSADOR DUKE!

BAM! BAM!

HAS THE STATE PREPARED ITS CASE?

WE HAVE, EXCELLENCY.

LOOKS IRONCLAD TO ME.

THANKS. SORRY ABOUT THE TYPOS.

NOW, *WAIT* A MINUTE!

GBTrudeau

"THE PEOPLE FURTHER CHARGE THAT MR. DUKE ENTERED THIS COUNTRY FOR THE EXPRESS PURPOSE OF ESPIONAGE AND BRIBERY."

WHAT IS THE DEFENSE OF THE ACCUSED?

HE MAINTAINS HE'S AN INNOCENT TOURIST.

IS THAT CORRECT, MR. DUKE?

MR. DUKE?

OH, SORRY, YOUR HONOR, I WAS JUST WRITING A FEW POSTCARDS.

GBTrudeau

THE DEFENDANT, AMBASSADOR DUKE, IS CHARGED HERE WITH HIGH CRIMES AGAINST GOD AND THE ISLAMIC REPUBLIC OF IRAN.

HE IS FURTHER ACCUSED OF ESPIONAGE, BRIBERY, ILLEGAL ENTRY AND POSSESSION OF DRUGS. THE PENALTY IN ALL CASES IS DEATH.

THE EVIDENCE IS OVERWHELMING. I FIND THE DEFENDANT GUILTY AS CHARGED!

WHAT? THE HELL I AM!

THE BAILIFF MAY FIRE WHEN READY.

OKAY, *OKAY!* I'M WILLING TO DEAL!

GBTrudeau

I JUST CAN'T BELIEVE JOANIE DIDN'T TELL ME ABOUT YOU. IT'S NOT LIKE HER AT ALL.

IMAGINE HAVING A SEVENTEEN-YEAR-OLD DAUGHTER AND NOT TELLING ANYONE!

IMAGINE BEING THE SEVENTEEN-YEAR-OLD DAUGHTER.

YEAH..

WELL, I GUESS WE BETTER CALL HER.

RIGHT! LET'S GET THIS GUILT TRIP ON THE ROAD!

HELLO, JOANIE? HI, IT'S ME..

LISTEN, THERE'S SOMEONE HERE AT THE APARTMENT TO SEE YOU. I THINK YOU OUGHT TO TALK TO HER..

HELLO, MOM?

SHE'S COMING RIGHT HOME!

IT'LL TAKE HER A WHILE. WHY DON'T YOU GO MAKE YOURSELF SOME BREAKFAST, AND I'LL MAKE UP THE SPARE ROOM..

OH, THAT WON'T BE NECESSARY, RICK. I'M NOT STAYING. I'M ON MY WAY TO COLLEGE.

COLLEGE? YOU MEAN, HERE IN WASHINGTON?

YUP. GEORGETOWN. I'LL BE STAYING IN THE DORMS. I'VE ALREADY BEEN AS-SIGNED A ROOMMATE AND EVERYTHING!

"JOAN CAUCUS, JR."?

WHERE IS SHE?

IN THE LIVING ROOM.

OH, RICK, I KNEW THIS WAS GOING TO HAVE TO HAPPEN SOONER OR LATER. I'M SO ASHAMED..

DO YOU THINK SHE HATES ME?

I DON'T KNOW. I GUESS SHE'D HAVE GOOD REASON.

YOU'RE MAD AT ME, TOO, AREN'T YOU, RICK?

ME? NOT AT ALL. LOOK, I'M PLAN-NING DINNER. GOT ANY OTHERS?

GOOD EVENING. TODAY "TIME" MAGAZINE PUBLISHED PART II OF THE MOST TRUMPETED MEMOIRS IN HISTORY— "HENRY KISSINGER, THE WHITEWASH YEARS."

AFTER A SUMMER OF FAWNING KISSINGER STORIES, "TIME" HAS FINALLY ARRIVED AT THE MAIN EVENT— AN ORGY OF EXCERPTS FROM A BOOK "TIME" ITSELF WILL PUBLISH..

IS THIS HOW THE RULING CLASS PROMOTES ITS OWN? I'M ROLAND HEDLEY. STAY WITH US FOR A LOOK AT WHAT HAPPENS WHEN A NEWS-WEEKLY DECIDES TO.. HYPE HENRY!

"HYPE HENRY: MEMOIRS ON THE MAKE," BROUGHT TO YOU BY THE CHASE MANHATTAN BANK..

"HYPE HENRY!" MEMOIRS ON THE MAKE
abc Special Report

G B Trudeau

HENRY KISSINGER'S "THE WHITE-WASH YEARS" IS NO ORDINARY BOOK. NOR IS "TIME" PROMOTING IT LIKE ONE. BILL WOOTEN, "TIME" MARKETING DIRECTOR, EXPLAINS.

WELL, WE STARTED SLOW, OF COURSE. WE RAN THE USUAL SEMIANNUAL KISSINGER PROFILES, REPORTS ON THE WORK-IN-PROGRESS, A FEW MENTIONS IN OUR "PEOPLE" SECTION..

THEN THIS SUMMER, WE POURED IT ON! AN EXCLUSIVE INTERVIEW, A FOUR-PAGE COLOR SPREAD ON HIS SALT LECTURE, TWO PAGES ON HIS NATO SPEECH! I MEAN, WE PUFFED OL' HENRY FROM HERE TO SUNDAY!

DO ANY NEWS STORIES?

UM.. WE MIGHT HAVE. THAT'S NOT MY DE-PARTMENT.

G B Trudeau

THE KISSINGER STORIES IN "TIME": LEGITIMATE COVERAGE OR ADEPT PROMOTION? WE ASKED HAMILTON LEFF, EDITOR OF THE MAGAZINE'S RESPECTED "NATION" SECTION..

MR. LEFF, IS IT TRUE THE PROMOTION DEPART-MENT ORCHESTRATED THE NONSTOP KISSINGER COVERAGE THIS SUMMER?

YES, THAT'S RIGHT.

IT IS?

THAT'S MY UNDERSTANDING.

AND THE "NATION" STAFF?

WE HANDLED THE PROOF-READING.

G B Trudeau

WHY ARE HENRY GRUNWALD AND THE OTHER EDITORS OF "TIME" SO INFATUATED WITH KISSINGER? NEW YORK SOCIAL CRITIC IRV BELL EXPLAINS.

OKAY, LOOK, THE GUY'S CLEARLY A WAR CRIMINAL, BUT WHEN YOU TALK ABOUT NAMES LIKE KISSINGER OR ROCKEFELLER OR BUNDY, YOU'RE TALKING INNER CIRCLE.

AT THAT LEVEL, THE FACT OF POWER AND ITS EFFECTIVE USE MEAN MUCH MORE THAN MERE MORAL CONSIDERATIONS. THE HEIRS OF HENRY LUCE UNDERSTAND THAT.

IS THERE ANYTHING THE AVERAGE GUY CAN DO ABOUT IT?

SURE. SPEAK OUT. CRASH THEIR DIN-NER PARTIES. ANY-THING TO KEEP THE PRESSURE ON.

G B Trudeau

POLITICAL MEMOIRS ARE NOTORIOUSLY SELF-SERVING, AND "WHITEWASH YEARS" IS NO EXCEPTION. SO IS THE BOOK OF ANY HISTORICAL VALUE? WE ASKED HISTORIAN LEO PARTCH.

WELL, IT'S HARD TO TELL, REALLY, BECAUSE THERE'S SO LITTLE IN THE LITERATURE TO WEIGH IT AGAINST.

SO FAR THE ONLY BOOKS ON KISSINGER HAVE BEEN WRITTEN BY OBSEQUIOUS T.V. CORRESPONDENTS WHO STILL TREMBLE AT THE HONOR OF ADDRESSING HIM BY HIS FIRST NAME.

FOR THE RECORD, THIS REPORTER HAS NEVER ENJOYED "HENRY" PRIVILEGES. BACK AFTER THIS.

AND SO THE BIG QUESTION AT TIME, INC., IS THIS: WILL SURVIVORS OF THE NIXON-KISSINGER ERA ACTUALLY BE TEMPTED TO PAY MONEY TO RELIVE IT?

700,000 WORDS. 1,521 PAGES. THE 30-MONTH OUTPUT OF KISSINGER'S HANDPICKED MEMOIR STAFF. BY ALMOST ANY STANDARD, "WHITEWASH YEARS" IS A VERY BIG BOOK!

GRANTED, HENRY KISSINGER HAD MUCH TO ANSWER FOR, BUT NEED SO MANY TREES HAVE DIED FOR THE CAUSE? MOST KISSINGER SCHOLARS THINK NOT.

HELL, IT ONLY TOOK ALBERT SPEER 520 PAGES..

THANK YOU, MR. WEINBURGER. ANY OTHER COMMENTS?

JOAN, JR?

HI! YOU MUST BE MY ROOMMATE, CHING!

ALL MY FRIENDS CALL ME HONEY.

PLEASED TO MEET YOU, HONEY. YOU CAN CALL ME J.J.

WELCOME TO COLLEGE, J.J.

THANK YOU.

I SUSPECT YOU WANT TO BE FILLED IN ON THE MEN SITUATION.

WELL, LET ME JUST GET RID OF THE PARENTS FIRST..

ANY WORD FROM YOUR BOYFRIEND YET, HONEY?

NO, AND I FEAR THE WORST.

I KNOW HE WOULDN'T WANT ME TO WORRY, BUT I CAN'T HELP IT. KHOMEINI'S PEOPLE ARE NOTHING BUT A GANG OF COMMON HOODLUMS!

KHOMEINI? WAIT A MINUTE! IS YOUR BOYFRIEND AMBASSADOR *DUKE?*

WE FELL IN LOVE IN THE EMBASSY COMPOUND. ALL OF PEKING WAS ABUZZ OVER IT..

WOW.. HOW ROMANTIC!

WE WERE TO BE MARRIED. I WAS GOING TO OPEN UP A LITTLE RESTAURANT IN DENVER.

WHAT'S IT SAY, ZONK?

"REGRET TO INFORM YOU YOUR UNCLE DUKE HAS BEEN DECLARED LEGALLY DEAD."

"READING OF WILL SCHEDULED FOR MONDAY. PLEASE COME SOONEST TO HELP ORGANIZE PERSONAL EFFECTS. CONDOLENCES. T. BANNON, ATTORNEY-AT-LAW."

GEE.. WHO DO YOU SUPPOSE MOVED TO HAVE HIM DECLARED LEGALLY DEAD?

I'M NOT SURE, BUT I'VE GOT A PRETTY GOOD IDEA!

YOU WANT THE STEREO PACKED TOO, BUDDY?

NO, NO, JUST PUT IT IN THE BACK OF MY VAN.

THIS SIDE UP ↑   FRAGILE

IS THAT YOU, BRENNER?

HEY, ZONK! GOOD TO SEE YOU AGAIN, MAN!

BRENNER, WHAT THE HELL IS GOING ON? WHO HAD DUKE DECLARED DEAD?

IT HAD TO BE DONE SOONER OR LATER, MAN. LIFE GOES ON, YOU KNOW?

SO YOU WROTE HIM OFF? JUST LIKE THAT?

WELL, WE WERE THINKING OF A MEMORIAL SERVICE, BUT HIS ATTORNEY AND I FIGURED WE OUGHTA TRY TO KEEP EXPENSES DOWN.

AS A COURTESY TO HIS HEIRS, NO DOUBT.

RIGHT. BESIDES, I COULDN'T REMEMBER WHICH CULT HE BELONGED TO.

GLAD YOU GOT HERE SO FAST, ZONK. THERE'S A LOT OF STUFF TO SORT THROUGH BEFORE THE WILL READING!

WHO'S COMING TO THE READING, BRENNER?

A PRETTY HEAVY CROWD, MAN. A GANG OF CREDITORS, A COUPLE IRS GUYS, AND A U.S. MARSHAL.

A U.S. MARSHAL?

NOT TO WORRY, MAN. I CHECKED IT OUT, AND MOST OF DUKE'S ESTATE IS INADMISSIBLE.

IMAGINE MY RELIEF.

ALL WE GOTTA DO IS GET THE SERIAL NUMBERS OFF.

FIND ANYTHING INTERESTING YET, MAN?

ARE YOU KIDDING? JUST LOOK AT ALL THIS STUFF!

PARKING TICKETS, EVICTION NOTICES, BETTING STUBS, FOOD STAMPS, BOUNCED CHECKS, REJECTION SLIPS, UNFINISHED MANUSCRIPTS, OVERDUE BILLS..

.. PRESCRIPTION BLANKS, FORGED PASSPORTS.. WHY, BRENNER, THERE'S A RECORD OF FAILURE AND MALFEASANCE HERE THAT SPANS OVER TWENTY YEARS!

YOU THINKING OF EDITING HIS PAPERS, MAN?

I DON'T KNOW IF I COULD DO IT JUSTICE!

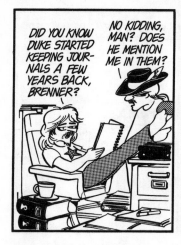

"APRIL 15, 1976. PEKING. INTENSE NEGOTIATIONS ON STATUS OF U.S./CHINA RELATIONS CONTINUE AT GREAT HALL OF THE PEOPLE.."

"TENG IS UNCOMPROMISING ON TAIWAN ISSUE. I MAKE NINE SEPARATE PROPOSALS, INCLUDING GENEROUS CASH SETTLEMENTS, PLUS POINTS. AM REBUKED AT EVERY TURN."

"APRIL 16. TENG REMAINS INTRACTABLE. IN ATTEMPT TO BREAK DEADLOCK, I CALL IN AIR STRIKES ON IMPERIAL PALACE."

"APRIL 17. PENTAGON OVERRULES STRIKES. AM LOSING FACE."

OKAY, IF EVERYONE HAS SOMETHING TO DRINK, I'D LIKE TO GET THIS SHOW ON THE ROAD.

I'M T.F. BANNON, COUNSEL FOR THE FIRM OF TORTS, TARTZ AND TORQUE, AND PERSONAL ATTORNEY FOR AMBASSADOR DUKE.

IT IS MY UNHAPPY TASK TO BE HERE TODAY TO READ THE WILL OF MR. DUKE, WHO IS.. UH.. PRESUMED DEAD AT THIS TIME.

STILL NO WORD FROM THE DECEASED YET, RIGHT?

NOT A PEEP, MAN. LET'S DO IT.

YOU A FRIEND OF THE FAMILY?

YOU MIGHT SAY THAT. I WORK FOR THE INTERNAL REVENUE SERVICE.

REALLY? HAVE YOU KNOWN DUKE LONG?

I WAS FIRST ASSIGNED TO HIS CASE IN 1963.

WOW..

HOW YOU BEARING UP?

NOT SO GOOD. IT'S SORT OF THE END OF AN ERA.

.."AND BEING OF ACCEPTABLY SOUND MIND AND WILL, I HEREBY LEAVE MY ENTIRE ESTATE TO.."

.."MY BELOVED PROTÉGÉ, MR. ZONKER HARRIS."

HUH?

OH, WOW..

YOU WERE HIS FAVORITE DEALER, I TAKE IT.

NO, NO, I'M AS SURPRISED AS YOU ARE!

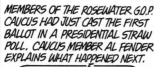

FOR THE CITIZENS OF ROSEWATER, THE MEDIA EVENT IS OVER. BUT THE SCARS LINGER ON. CAUCUS MEMBER SHELLY SIMMS SHARES HER TRAUMA AND SHAME.

WELL, I WAS JUST LEAVING THE VFW HALL WHEN I FIRST SAW THEM. I TRIED TO FLEE, BUT THERE WERE TOO MANY OF THEM. A BIG ONE, WITH A MICROPHONE, CORNERED ME..

I TRIED TO RESIST, I TRIED TO TELL HIM IT WAS JUST A STRAW POLL, THAT IT DIDN'T MEAN ANYTHING, BUT HE..HE..

HE WHAT, MS. SIMMS?

HE INTER-VIEWED ME! REPEAT-EDLY!

WHO, MS. SIMMS? WHO DID THIS TO YOU? WAS IT ROGER MUDD?

NOW THAT THE MEDIA CIRCUS HAS LEFT TOWN, THE VICTIMS OF THIS SENSE-LESS, MINDLESS COVERAGE MUST TRY TO PICK UP THE PIECES. HOMEMAKER DOTTY HOLMES TALKS OF HER DESPAIR.

IT'S HARDEST ON MY THREE KIDS. THEY'RE HEARTBROKEN. THEY KEEP ASKING ME, "MOMMY, WHEN ARE THE T.V. PEOPLE COMING BACK?"

I DON'T KNOW WHAT WE'LL DO. ABC NEWS PROMISED US THERE'D BE A FOLLOW-UP STORY, BUT WE DON'T HAVE MUCH HOPE THAT ANYTHING WILL COME OF IT..

THIS IS THE FOLLOW-UP STORY, MRS. HOLMES.

OH. WELL, IT'S JUST NOT THE SAME.

HELLO?

HELLO, MS. CAUCUS? THIS IS MS. HUAN, J.J.'S ROOM-MATE..

WHY, YES, HOW ARE YOU, DEAR?

FINE, THANKS. J.J. ASKED ME TO CALL YOU AND TELL YOU SHE JUST LEFT FOR YOUR PLACE..

SHE HAS TO MEET HER BOYFRIEND ZEKE AT THE AIRPORT, THOUGH, SO SHE'LL ONLY HAVE ABOUT TEN MINUTES FOR DINNER..

WELL, WE'LL CERTAINLY BE LOOKING FOR-WARD TO THAT, DEAR..

SHE DOESN'T WANT ANY-THING FANCY. JUST A LIGHT SALAD.

HI, RICK. LOOK, I HAVE TO MEET ZEKE AT THE AIRPORT, SO I CAN'T STAY FOR VERY LONG..

IT'S PROBABLY JUST AS WELL. MOM'S BEEN ON MY CASE A LOT LATELY, WHICH I'M NOT SURE SHE'S ENTI-TLED TO. YOU GUYS HAVEN'T BEEN FIGHTING, HAVE YOU?

LISTEN, WHEN I BRING ZEKE BY AFTER DINNER, TRY NOT TO BE TOO JUDGMENTAL, OKAY? HE'S A LIBRA AND VERY SENSITIVE.

HI, JOAN. WON'T YOU COME IN?

OH, MOM! YOU'RE NOT SERVING MEAT!

A FOOTNOTE'S PROGRESS

Q: You have been accused by numerous political observers of aiding and abetting the Anderson campaign. How do you plead?

A: Puzzlement. Anyone dumb enough to get his political information from a comic strip deserves what he gets at the polls. The Anderson strips were perceived as kindly, and thus an endorsement. The candidate's own view of the cartoon connection changed from week to week. At first he was disturbed, then he started quoting the strip in every speech. Later, both he and his campaign manager repudiated it.[1] It made it very hard for the public to keep abreast of the impact I was supposed to be having. In the end, I think I only swayed about three or four million votes, although which way I can't be sure.

[1] Anderson's final assessment: "I don't regard *Doonesbury* as the apotheosis of what the John Anderson campaign is all about."

MR. AFSHAR, COULD YOU COMMENT ON THE REPORT THAT SEVERAL OF YOUR FELLOW TERRORISTS ARE NO LONGER IN GOOD ACADEMIC STANDING?

THESE LIES ARE AS FOUL AND NOXIOUS AS THE SPUTUM OF A CAMEL. WE ARE ALL TRUE BELIEVERS, AND WE CAN ONLY FAIL IF ALLAH WILLS IT.

THE ACADEMIC PRESSURE THAT DOES EXIST IS QUITE NORMAL. NATURALLY, EACH OF US IS ANXIOUS TO TAKE HIS PLACE IN THE NEW ISLAMIC SOCIETY. WITH 40% UNEMPLOYMENT, SOME COMPETITION IS INEVITABLE.

ANY CHEATING?

VERY LITTLE. ONLY AMONG THE PREMEDS.

GBTrudeau

MR. AFSHAR, WHAT IS YOUR REACTION TO THE REPORT THAT STUDENTS WITH THE WORST ACADEMIC PROBLEMS HAVE BEEN ROTATED FROM DUTY?

THESE FALSEHOODS FESTER IN THE MOUTHS OF ZIONIST JACK-RABBITS. THE STUDENTS WHO LED THIS MOST HOLY ATTACK ARE STILL WITHIN THE COMPOUND.

WE HAVE REMAINED AT OUR POSTS THROUGHOUT, EVEN ON THE FIRST SATURDAY OF DECEMBER, WHICH IS, OF COURSE, SACRED TO US.

SACRED? HOW SO?

HOMECOMING. THE BIG SOCCER GAME WITH QOM TECH.

GBTrudeau

HEY, ZONKER, YOU GOT AN OVERNIGHT BAG?

UNDER MY BED. YOU GOING SOMEWHERE?

WELL, IF I CAN TALK MIKE OUT OF HIS CAR, I'D LIKE TO GO HOME TOMORROW. IS HE AROUND?

IN THE KITCHEN. HE'S WORKING ON A DATE FOR NEW YEAR'S.

STILL?

THESE THINGS TAKE TIME.

YES?

HI, YOU DON'T KNOW ME, BUT I SAW YOUR PICTURE IN THE STUDENT DIRECTORY, AND I..

GBTrudeau

TEN!.. NINE!..

EIGHT!.. SEVEN!.. SIX!..

FIVE!.. FOUR!.. THREE!..

HI, YOU DON'T KNOW ME, BUT..

OKAY, NOW, TRY NOT TO SOUND DESPERATE.

GBTrudeau

GOOD MORNIN', FRIENDS. I'M JOHN CONNALLY, AND I WANT TO WELCOME YOU TO FEST, THE FREE ENTERPRISE TRAININ' SEMINAR.

HERE AT FEST, WE LIKE TO THINK THAT RICH IS BETTER. SO WE TRY TO SHOW FOLKS HOW TO TURN OFF THE GUILT. WE SHOW 'EM THAT IT'S OKAY TO SUCCEED, THAT BUSINESS IS BEAUTIFUL.

THAT'S ALL THERE IS TO IT, FRIENDS. FOR THE NEXT 48 HOURS, YOU'RE SIMPLY GONNA LEARN TO TAKE RESPONSIBILITY FOR YOUR OWN WEALTH. ANY QUESTIONS?

YEAH, THIS ISN'T ONE OF THOSE DEALS WHERE WE CAN'T GO TO THE JOHN, IS IT?

HELL, NO! YOU'RE RICH! YOU CAN DO WHATEVER YOU WANT!

YOU'RE NOT HERE FOR DOUBLE-TALK, GENTLEMEN. YOU'RE HERE BECAUSE, AS BUSINESSMEN, YOU'RE SICK AND TIRED OF BEING BLAMED FOR ALL OF SOCIETY'S ILLS!

YOU KNOW THAT AS AMERICA'S CAPTAINS OF INDUSTRY, YOU DESERVE BETTER. YOU KNOW THAT AS OUR LAST LINE OF DEFENSE AGAINST CHEAP JAPANESE IMPORTS, YOU DESERVE OUR RESPECT!

THE CONNALLY WAY OFFERS YOU THAT RESPECT. IT GIVES YOU THE SPACE IN WHICH TO REALIZE YOUR EARNING POTENTIAL. IT SAYS THAT TAX INCENTIVES ARE OKAY. AND BY DEREGULATING INDUSTRY, IT CREATES A CONTEXT FOR GROWTH.

I FEEL BETTER ABOUT MYSELF ALREADY.

ME, TOO.

WE CALL IT "GETTING YOURS."

THAT'S THE BOTTOM LINE, FRIENDS. SIMPLY PUT, THE CONNALLY APPROACH SPEAKS TO THE DREAMS OF THE AVERAGE EXECUTIVE, THE NEGLECTED MAN AT THE TOP.

THINK ABOUT IT. YOU, MR. SLACKMEYER, YOU MUST HAVE A DREAM, SOME PRIVATE YEARNING YOU'VE ALWAYS BEEN AFRAID TO EXPRESS..

WELL, YEAH, AS A MATTER OF FACT, I HAVE. IT CONCERNS ENVIRONMENTAL STANDARDS..

YES?

SOMETIMES I FANTASIZE ABOUT RELAXING THEM.

RELAXIN' 'EM? HELL, WHY NOT PUT 'EM TO SLEEP?

GOVERNOR, WHAT DO YOU DO ABOUT PRESSURE FROM FAMILY AND FRIENDS? FOR INSTANCE, MY WIFE IS ALWAYS CRITICIZING ME FOR PRICE GOUGING.

WELL, FIRST OF ALL, YOU MUST EXPLAIN TO YOUR LITTLE GAL THAT THERE'S NO SUCH THING AS PRICE GOUGING. IT'S CALLED SUPPLY AND DEMAND.

THEN YOU GOTTA REMIND HER IT'S A ROUGH WORLD OUT THERE. AS I'VE SAID BEFORE, EVERYBODY'S HUMAN. THERE'S A LITTLE LARCENY IN THE HEARTS OF ALL OF US.

"US," GOVERNOR?

WELL, NOT ME. I WAS ACQUITTED. BUT STILL, IT'S QUITE NORMAL.

GOVERNOR, YOU TALK ABOUT NOT LETTING OUR-SELVES BE VICTIMIZED, HOW CAN WE AVOID IT WHEN OUR STREETS AREN'T SAFE TO WALK ON?

GOOD QUESTION, MR. ANDREWS. HOW **CAN** WE AVOID IT? WELL, WE COULD BEGIN BY MAKIN' DARN SURE THE CRIMINAL ELEMENTS AREN'T ON THE STREETS IN THE FIRST PLACE!

YOU TAKE YOUR WOULD-BE MUGGER. JUST HOW DETERRED DO YOU FIGURE HE IS BY THE THREAT OF A SUSPENDED SENTENCE?

NOT AT ALL.

RIGHT. NOW, SAY HE KNEW HE'D BE ELECTROCUTED ON TELEVISION?

WELL, THAT WOULD DEPEND IN PART ON THE RATINGS, WOULDN'T IT?

HI, IT'S RICK. IS HE THERE YET?

UH-HUH. HE AND JOAN JUST ARRIVED.

SO WHAT'S HE LIKE?

WELL, HIS NAME IS ZEKE. ZEKE BRENNER. HE'S FROM ASPEN, COLORADO.

AND?

WELL, HE'S QUITE..QUITE SOMETHING.

I DON'T THINK SHE LIKES ME, MAN.

WHAT ARE YOU TALKING ABOUT? SHE **ADORES** YOU!

JOAN SAYS YOU'RE A CARETAKER, ZEKE. THAT MUST BE INTERESTING.

YEAH, IT IS, MAN.

A LOT OF PEOPLE DON'T APPRECIATE CUSTODIAL WORK, BUT IT'S REALLY VERY CHALLENGING. YOU GOTTA BE PRETTY SHARP, YOU KNOW?

I CAN IMAGINE. BUT DOES IT PAY WELL ENOUGH FOR YOU TO SUPPORT BOTH YOURSELF AND JOAN?

OH, WELL, I DEAL A LITTLE DOPE, TOO.

MOTHER! STOP BEING SO NOSEY!

SO HOW LONG HAVE YOU BEEN A CARETAKER, ZEKE?

I GUESS IT'S BEEN ABOUT THREE YEARS, MAN.

IS IT SOMETHING YOU'RE PURSUING AS A CAREER?

NO, NO, IT'S JUST TEMPORARY UNTIL THE RIGHT OPPORTUNITY COMES ALONG.

I GOT A GOOD JOB OFFER WORKIN' ON A CONSTRUCTION SITE IN DENVER RECENTLY, BUT, OF COURSE, I HAD TO TURN IT DOWN.

YOU HAD TO?

I'M TOO SENSITIVE, MAN.

ZEKE'S A LIBRA, MOM.

SENATOR KENNEDY, DO YOU AGREE WITH YOUR FELLOW CANDIDATES THAT THE PRESIDENT HAS MISHANDLED THE CRISIS IN AFGHANISTAN?

WELL, IN THIS MOMENT OF NATIONAL CRISIS, ANY SECOND-GUESSING THAT I.. ER..PERSONALLY, WITH RESPECT TO THE INTERESTS OF PEACE.

MOREOVER, WITH THE.. UH.. UNCHALLENGED SOVIET THREAT, THE.. ER..GRAIN EMBARGO WHICH..UH.. AS FAR AS STRONG LEADERSHIP IN THIS COUNTRY!

NOW, IN RESPECT TO THE..

A VERB, SENATOR, WE NEED A VERB!

GBTrudeau

GOVERNOR BROWN, DO YOU THINK PRESIDENT CARTER WAS RIGHT TO RULE OUT A MILITARY STRIKE TO FREE THE HOSTAGES IN TEHRAN?

ABSOLUTELY NOT. NO OPTION SHOULD EVER BE RULED OUT. ESPECIALLY IN THE FACE OF A SERIOUS THREAT TO THE VIABILITY OF STARSHIP AMERICA.

FOREIGN POLICY HAS TO BE VIEWED AS PROCESS. UNDER CERTAIN CIRCUMSTANCES, A MILITARY POSTURE SHOULD BE PERMITTED TO EVOLVE.

WHAT SORT OF REACTION TIME ARE WE TALKING HERE, GOVERNOR?

WHATEVER FEELS RIGHT.

GBTrudeau

GENTLEMEN, ALL OF YOU HAVE BEEN EXTREMELY CRITICAL OF PRESIDENT CARTER'S ACTIONS, BUT NO ONE HAS SAID WHAT HE WOULD HAVE DONE DIFFERENTLY..

EACH OF YOU HAS IMPLIED THAT SOME SORT OF DIRECT MILITARY ACTION MIGHT HAVE BEEN IN ORDER. DOES ANYONE CARE TO GO ON THE RECORD AS ADVOCATING THAT? SENATOR BAKER?

MR. REDFERN, I'M AFRAID I CAN'T ANSWER THAT QUESTION. THIS TIME NEXT YEAR I EXPECT TO BE PRESIDENT, AND I'D RATHER NOT TIP MY HAND TO THE SOVIETS.

SAME HERE.

ME, TOO.

SORRY. GOOD QUESTION, THOUGH.

THANKS.

GBTrudeau

HEY, MARCUS, GUESS WHAT I JUST HEARD ON THE RADIO! JOHN ANDERSON IS GIVING A MAJOR CAMPAIGN SPEECH ON CAMPUS TONIGHT!

I KNOW. MIKE JUST WENT IN TO SEE HIM.

HOW EXCITING! MAYBE WE SHOULD GO, TOO!

YOU LIKE ANDERSON?

UM.. I DON'T KNOW. WHO IS HE?

I'D LIKE TO THANK ALL OF YOU FOR TURNING OUT TONIGHT..

MONDAY NIGHTS ARE ALWAYS BAD, SIR. IT'S NOT YOUR FAULT.

GBTrudeau

WELL, I GUESS WE BETTER GET STARTED..

MR. ANDERSON, I'D LIKE TO APOLOGIZE FOR THE POOR TURN-OUT TONIGHT. MONDAY NIGHTS ARE **ALWAYS** BAD HERE.

ALSO, THERE'S A BIG BASKET-BALL GAME WITH COLUMBIA TONIGHT. EVERYBODY, BUT EVERY-BODY, GOES TO THE COLUMBIA GAME. IT'S CONSIDERED PRETTY DE RIGUEUR.

SO, REALLY, IT'S NO REFLECTION ON YOUR CAMPAIGN. IT'S JUST A SCHEDULING CONFLICT. THE STUDENTS ALL BOUGHT TICKETS TO THE GAME MONTHS AGO, SO WHAT COULD THEY DO?

I SEE. WELL, THANK YOU FOR EX-PLAINING.

ALSO, WE'RE IN THE MIDDLE OF AN ANNETTE FUNICELLO FILM FESTIVAL. IT'S JUST BAD TIMING.

INEXPLICABLY, WE STILL PAY TRIBUTE TO THE EXTORTION-IST DEMANDS OF OPEC. INSTEAD OF PERMITTING THEM THE PRIVILEGE, WE SHOULD BE WILLING TO TAX CONSUMPTION OF GAS IN THIS COUNTRY!

WOW..

CONGRESSMAN ANDERSON, THAT'S ONE OF THE MORE AUDACIOUS PRO-POSALS OF THE YEAR. AND YET, BECAUSE YOU ARE SO UNCOMMONLY WELL-SPOKEN, THE IDEA SEEMS TO MAKE A GREAT DEAL OF SENSE.

THANK YOU.

YOU HAVE QUITE A GIFT, SIR.. WHAT DO YOU EXPECT TO DO WITH IT?

RUN FOR PRESIDENT.

OH, RIGHT. SORRY. CARRY ON.

NOW MORE THAN EVER, WE MUST NOT PERMIT OURSELVES TO BE OVERCOME WITH A NEW MISSILE MADNESS, A MINDLESS RENEWAL OF UNRESTRICTED COMPETITION.

BEFORE IT IS TOO LATE, WE MUST MOVE TO RATIFY SALT. SALT IS NOT A UNILATERAL FAVOR WE ARE DOING THE SOVIET UNION; WE SHOULD NOT BE PENALIZING OURSELVES FOR SOVIET BEHAVIOR!

EXCUSE ME, CONGRESSMAN ANDERSON, BUT ARE YOU **SURE** YOU'RE A REPUBLI-CAN? YOU SURE DON'T **SOUND** LIKE A RE-PUBLICAN!

GREAT.

HEY, BUT WHAT DO I KNOW? I'M A DEMOCRAT.

YES, IT WILL TAKE MORE THAN HORTATORY EXPRESSIONS ABOUT LEADERSHIP TO RESTORE OUR FLAGGING NATIONAL FORTUNES. THAT'S WHY I'M RUNNING AND THAT'S WHY I NEED YOUR SUPPORT!

BRAVO! YEAA!

CLAP! CLAP! CLAP!

WE WANT ANDERSON! WE WANT ANDERSON!

STOMP! STOMP!

THANK YOU. COULD YOU TELL ME HOW TO GET TO THE BUS STATION?

SURE. DO YOU NEED A LIFT?

 HOW DID THE LEGISLATORS GATHER ENOUGH EVIDENCE TO BUST UP THE FBI ENTRAPMENT RING? I ASKED ONE OF THE CONGRESSMEN INVOLVED..

 PIECE OF CAKE, REALLY. I SIMPLY PUT OUT THE WORD I WAS OPEN TO A BRIBE. THE RUSE WORKED LIKE A CHARM. WITHIN DAYS, I WAS BEING HANDED $50,000 IN TAXPAYERS' MONEY!

 IN THE WEEKS THAT FOLLOWED, THE SCOPE OF MY INVESTIGATION WIDENED. TO MY SHOCK, I WAS OFFERED BRIBES BY AGENTS IN NEW JERSEY, NEW YORK, FLORIDA, EVEN TEXAS!

 CONGRESSMAN, DID YOU FIND ANY HONEST FBI AGENTS? ONLY ONE. BUT HE WAS GREAT. HE WOULDN'T GIVE ME A DIME.

 IF THIS SCANDAL HAS A HERO, THEN SURELY IT IS ARMSTRONG ALGER, THE ONLY FBI AGENT TO REFUSE TO ENTRAP AN UNDERCOVER CONGRESSMAN. ALGER DESCRIBED THE ENCOUNTER TO ABC NEWS.

 ACTUALLY IT WAS VERY BRIEF. HE SIMPLY TURNED UP AT THE HOUSE ONE NIGHT, SAID HE HAD HEARD ABOUT THE BRIBES AND WANTED A PIECE OF THE ACTION.

 I REPLIED IT WAS UNETHICAL FOR ME TO ENTICE HIM INTO COMMITTING A CRIME HE WOULDN'T NORMALLY CONSIDER. THEN HE BECAME MAD AND STOMPED OUT OF THE HOUSE.

 SO YOU DIDN'T GIVE HIM ANY MONEY AT ALL? HE JUST WASN'T PREDISPOSED ENOUGH. LATER, HE CALLED TO CONGRATULATE ME.

 WHAT WAS IT LIKE LIVING NEXT DOOR TO AN FBI ENTRAPMENT RING? NEIGHBOR WILBER FILBIS TALKED TO ABC WIDE WORLD OF NEWS ABOUT HIS ORDEAL..

 LISTEN, I GOT THREE KIDS. IT'S HARD ENOUGH KEEPING THEM AWAY FROM PUSHERS AT THE PLAYGROUND WITHOUT HAVING TO WORRY ABOUT WHITE COLLAR CRIME NEXT DOOR!

 IT'S SORT OF CREEPY, Y'KNOW? JUST KNOWING THAT RIGHT ACROSS THE STREET, PEOPLE WERE BEING INDUCED TO COMMIT CRIMES WITHOUT ANY PREDISPOSITION AT ALL!

 EVER HEAR ANY SCREAMS? NO, BUT WE KNEW THEY WERE BAD NEWS. THEY ALL CARRIED GUNS AND NEVER CAME TO BLOCK PARTIES.

 FOR THE SPECIAL TEAM OF INVESTIGATING CONGRESSMEN, OPERATION "CONSCAM" IS OVER. ITS MISSION HAS BEEN COMPLETED.

 BUT FOR ATTORNEY GENERAL BENJAMIN CIVILETTI AND THE SCORES OF FBI OFFICIALS IMPLICATED IN THE ENTRAPMENT SCANDAL, THE NIGHTMARE HAS JUST BEGUN.

 TODAY AS HEARINGS GOT UNDER WAY, CONGRESSMEN CAME FORWARD ONE BY ONE TO TELL HORROR STORIES OF BEING WANTONLY HOUNDED INTO ACCEPTING MONEY THEY WANTED NO PART OF.

 COUNTER-CHARGES THAT THEY TOOK THE BRIBES WILLINGLY ARE BEING LAUGHED OFF. THIS IS ROLAND HEDLEY.

COMING UP, TANNING ACE ZONKER HARRIS..

..WITH A FULL REPORT ON THE FORT LAUDERDALE SUN SPRINTS!

TODAY ON "PROFILES ON PARADE," WE'RE DELIGHTED TO WELCOME TANNING EXPERT ZONKER HARRIS. ZONKER, I UNDERSTAND YOU'RE JUST BACK FROM THE FORT LAUDERDALE SUN SPRINTS.

THAT'S RIGHT, MARK, I WAS THERE COMPETING ON A COPPERTONE FELLOWSHIP. AS PART OF THE PROGRAM, I'LL ALSO BE TRAVELING TO CALIFORNIA THIS SUMMER, TO STUDY UNDER THE GREAT TANMASTER GEORGE HAMILTON AT HIS WORKSHOP IN MALIBU.

THAT'S QUITE AN HONOR. HOW DO YOU GET SELECTED FOR A FELLOWSHIP?

WELL, YOU HAVE TO SUBMIT A PORTFOLIO OF COLOR SLIDES, ALONG WITH AFFIDAVITS FROM YOUR DERMATOLOGIST.

DO YOU REGARD THIS AS A CAREER MOVE? WHAT SORT OF PROSPECTS DO YOU FACE AS A TRAINED TANNIST?

WELL, MARK, THERE IS A GROWING NUMBER OF OPPORTUNITIES IN THE AREA OF SHOW TANNING, BUT FULL-TIME EMPLOYMENT IS STILL PRETTY SCARCE.

IN FACT, GEORGE HIMSELF IS PROBABLY THE ONLY PERSON TO EVER PARLAY A TAN INTO A WHOLE CAREER, ALTHOUGH HE **HAS** PLACED SEVERAL GRADUATES FROM HIS CLINIC ON "HOLLYWOOD SQUARES."

THAT'S THE ONLY SHOW WHICH TAKES TAN PEOPLE?

WELL, IT'S THE ONLY ONE WHICH ACTUALLY **PAYS** YOU TO BE TAN.

GBTrudeau

TAP! TAP! TAP! TAP!

GOOD NEWS, MAN. WE'VE STARTED THE ACTUAL WRITING. I THINK IT'S TIME YOU PUT OUT THE WORD TO PUBLISHERS.

TAP! TAP! TAP! TAP!

I'LL GET RIGHT ON IT, ZEKE. DO YOU HAVE ANY PREF-ERENCES IN PA-PERBACK HOUSES?

TAP! TAP! TAP! TAP!

NO, JUST SO LONG AS IT'S A CLASSY OUTFIT. I MEAN, I'VE GOT AN IMPORTANT STORY TO TELL HERE. WE'RE NOT JUST OUT TO MAKE A FAST BUCK.

FINISHED!

TALK TO YOU LATER, MAN. I GOTTA GO HELP WITH THE FOOT-NOTES.

I'M REALLY IMPRESSED, MAN. THIS IS JUST A FIRST-CLASS JOB!

WELL, GIVEN THE TIME CONSTRAINTS..

I MEAN, YOU NEVER EVEN MET THE GUY, AND YOU CAPTURED HIM PERFECTLY!

"DUKE. HE WAS ONE OF A KIND, AN ORIGINAL. HE SHOT FROM THE HIP, STOOD IN NO MAN'S SHADOW, NEVER TOOK NO FOR AN ANSWER, ALWAYS WENT THE DISTANCE, AND LIVED AND DIED BY THE SWORD."

I'D LOVE TO STAY AND POLISH, BUT..

ARE YOU KIDDING? THIS IS TERRIFIC!

J.J.! IT'S HIM.

WHO?.. ZEKE!

HI, DOLL! JUST GOT IN. PACK YOUR BAGS. WE'RE GOING TO BERMUDA.

BERMUDA? ZEKE, WHAT ARE YOU TALKING ABOUT?

I FINISHED MY BOOK ON DUKE. BANTAM IS PUBLISHING IT, AND I'M GETTING AN AD-VANCE OF $100,000!

DUKE? YOU WROTE A BOOK ON DUKE? WHAT DO YOU SAY ABOUT HIM?

UM.. I DUNNO. I HAVEN'T HAD A CHANCE TO READ IT YET.

$100,000! IT MUST BE REALLY GOOD!

SO THE BOOK SHOULD BE IN THE STORES IN A MATTER OF WEEKS. NATURALLY, THERE'LL BE A BIG BOOK TOUR.

A BOOK TOUR? WOW!

IT'S ALL SO EXCITING, ZEKE! LET'S GO OVER AND TELL MOTHER RIGHT AWAY!

YOUR MOTHER? WHAT FOR, MAN?

BECAUSE THIS'LL SHOW HER THAT WE REALLY DO HAVE A FUTURE. WE COULD EVEN PICK A DATE NOW!

SHOULDN'T YOU PUT TOGETHER A FIVE-YEAR PLAN FIRST?

THAT WOULD BE DISHONEST, HONEY. ZEKE AND I DON'T BELIEVE IN QUOTAS.

MOM?

WELL, HELLO, DEAR. HOW'S EVERYTHING GOING?

MOM, GO TURN ON T.V.! CHANNEL TWO! ZEKE'S ON "DINAH" TALKING ABOUT DUKE!

"DINAH"? ZEKE'S ON THE DINAH SHORE SHOW?

THEN HE WOULD ADD TWO TABLE-SPOONS OF ETHER..

MMM! IT SOUNDS WONDERFUL!

MY DEAR MR. BRENNER.

MY DEAR MR. CAVETT.

I HAVE THE STRANGEST FEEL-ING THAT WE'VE MET BEFORE. PERHAPS AT A STOKOWSKI CONCERT, OR MAYBE AT GROUCHO'S HOUSE?

BEATS ME, MAN.

TELL ME, IS IT TRUE YOU KNEW THE BARRYMORES? OR AM I THINKING OF SOMEONE ELSE I MET AT PAUL SIMON'S NEW YORK LIBRARY BENEFIT? HOW PECULIAR. NO MATTER.

SOME MORE SHERRY?

NO, THANKS. LISTEN, COULD WE PICK THIS UP A LITTLE? I'M BEGINNING TO NOD OFF.

I DON'T BELIEVE THIS. THEY'VE SENT ME EIGHT CASES OF VOD-KA FOR TONIGHT.

I THOUGHT YOU'D SWORN OFF OF RE-UNION DUTY, MARCUS.

I DON'T HAVE ANY CHOICE. DAD'S IM-POSED A SPENDING CEILING ON MY EDU-CATION THIS YEAR.

THAT'S AN OUTRAGE! HOW COULD HE DO THAT TO YOU?

WELL, FOR ONE THING, A YEAR HERE NOW COSTS $8,000.

IT DOESN'T HAVE TO. JUST CUT OUT THE EXTRAS, MAN. WHY, I'M ONLY PAYING $3,400!

UH-HUH. WHAT SORT OF EXTRAS ARE WE TALK-ING ABOUT, ZONK?!

WELL, LIKE TUITION. I FIND THAT I CAN MAKE DO WITHOUT CLASSES.

MAN, I CAN'T BE-LIEVE IT! ONLY FIVE YEARS OUT, AND ALL MY CLASSMATES ARE EITHER DOCTORS OR LAWYERS!

SO WHAT'S WRONG WITH THAT, FELLAH? WHAT DO YOU DO?

I HAVE A LITTLE HEAD SHOP PARA-PHERNALIA BUSINESS.

UH-HUH. EVER REGRET NOT CHOOSING LAW OR MEDICINE YOURSELF?

NO.. NO, NOT REALLY.

SURE ABOUT THAT, SON?

I THINK SO. I'M WORTH ABOUT FIVE MILLION NOW.

HELLO.

WELL, SURE, BUT WITH INFLATION, WHO ISN'T?

THE POINT I WANT TO MAKE HERE IS THAT I THINK IT'S TIME WE PUT BEHIND US THE DISCREDITED POLICIES OF FEDERAL HANDOUTS!

THE WELFARE STATE HAS BROUGHT NOTHING BUT MORAL DECAY. TIME AND AGAIN, THE WELFARE SYSTEM HAS LED DIRECTLY TO CRIME AND THE DISSOLUTION OF FAMILIES.

GOVERNOR REAGAN, DO YOU HAVE ANY EVIDENCE FOR SUCH A CLAIM?

CERTAINLY. I REFER YOU TO ONE REPORT I HAVE HERE FROM THE "NEW YORK DAILY NEWS" OF MAY 2, 1953..

1953?

"NAB WELFARE MOM IN BABY AXING.."

MR. REDFERN?

TAP! TAP!

YO.

YOU GAVE THE GOVERNOR A PRETTY HARD TIME TODAY ABOUT HIS FACTS. HE'D LIKE A CHANCE TO SHOW YOU WHERE HE GOT THEM.

TAP! TAP!

YOU MEAN, HE DIDN'T JUST MAKE THEM UP?

OF COURSE NOT. THEY'RE FROM HIS PERSONAL LIBRARY OF OVER 10,000 PRESS CLIPPINGS. HE'D LOVE YOU TO COME UP TO HIS SUITE AND SEE IT.

THE MAN TRAVELS WITH 10,000 PRESS CLIPPINGS?

WE KEEP 'EM IN SHOE BOXES. HIS CURATOR DOESN'T LIKE TO BREAK UP THE COLLECTION.

HIGGINS!

YEAH, BOSS?

WHERE THE HELL IS REDFERN? WE CLOSE IN AN HOUR, AND I DON'T HAVE HIS REAGAN PIECE!

HE CALLED IN TO SAY HE'S WORKING ON AN EXCLUSIVE, BOSS. REAGAN'S SHOWING HIM HIS CLIPPING COLLECTION.

HIS WHAT?

.. AND THOSE ARE MY PRIZE "RED MENACE" CLIPS FROM "BOY'S LIFE"..

YOU CERTAINLY HAVE SOME BEAUTIES HERE, SIR.

SO YOU SEE, MR. REDFERN, WHEN I USE FACTS AND FIGURES, I'VE GOT THE DOCUMENTATION TO BACK THEM UP WITH.

WHAT YOU SEE IN FRONT OF YOU IS A LIFETIME OF CAREFUL RESEARCH. FROM "TV GUIDE" TO "READER'S DIGEST" TO THE LEADING AIRLINE MAGAZINES, I'VE LEFT NO PAGE UNTURNED.

THESE ARE MY "RIGHT TO LIFE" CLIPPINGS, OVER THERE IS "GUN CONTROL," "THE SOVIET THREAT," AND THE BOX YOU'VE GOT IS.. UH..

IT SAYS "LEAGUE OF NATIONS."

OH.. WELL, ACTUALLY, THAT ONE'S RETIRED.

"WILSON TO SIGN TREATY AT VERSAILLES." BOY, SURE TAKES YOU BACK, DOESN'T IT, SIR?

..AND WHILE IT'S TRUE THAT SOME OF MY CLIPPINGS FROM "LIBERTY" AND "COLLIER'S" ARE A BIT DATED, MOST OF THEM HAVE AS MUCH SIGNIFICANCE FOR US NOW AS THEY DID IN THE '30'S.

FOR EXAMPLE, DID YOU KNOW THIS? "STUDIES NOW SHOW THAT NEARLY 95% OF ALL PEOPLE ON THE PUBLIC DOLE ROUTINELY TURN DOWN HONEST WORK WHEN IT IS OFFERED TO THEM."

THAT'S VERY INTERESTING, GOVERNOR. YOU REALIZE, OF COURSE, THAT THAT'S UTTERLY PREPOSTEROUS.

I ONLY KNOW WHAT I READ.

YES, SIR. I THINK THAT'S WHAT'S GOT EVERYONE SO CONCERNED.

UM..OKAY, YOU GUYS ALL KNOW ME. I'M BROOKS HARKNESS, PRESIDENT OF THE SIXTH FORM..

TODAY WE AT ST. GROTTLESEX PREP ARE PRIVILEGED TO WELCOME PRESIDENTIAL CANDIDATE GEORGE BUSH, ANDOVER '42, AND YALE '48!

AMBASSADOR BUSH, IF I MAY, I'D LIKE TO ASK THE FIRST QUESTION..

FABULOUS! LET'S GET A DIALOGUE GOING HERE!

WHAT WOULD YOU DO TO MAKE GOVERNMENT LESS TACKY?

I'D DO LOADS! THIS IS A GREAT COUNTRY! GOVERNMENT DOESN'T HAVE TO BE TACKY!

AMBASSADOR BUSH, HAS BEING A PREPPIE HURT YOUR CAREER?

ON THE CONTRARY! I'VE FOUND THAT WHEN GIVEN A CHOICE, PEOPLE ACTUALLY PREFER TO VOTE PREPPIE!

AND WHY NOT? WE'VE GOT THE TRACK RECORD! WHY, OUR GREAT BOARDING SCHOOLS AND IVY LEAGUE COLLEGES HAVE ALWAYS PRODUCED MORE THAN THEIR FAIR SHARE OF LEADERS!

THINK ABOUT IT! WHAT DID SUCH GREAT PRESIDENTS AS WOODROW WILSON, FRANKLIN ROOSEVELT AND JOHN KENNEDY ALL HAVE IN — COMMON?

THEY ALL GOT US INTO WAR?

RIGHT! THESE SCHOOLS JUST DON'T TURN OUT SISSIES!

AMBASSADOR BUSH, DO YOU FAVOR FEDERAL GUARANTEES ON SUMMER VACATION LOANS?

GOSH, YES!

I THINK WE HAVE A SERIOUS YOUTH PROBLEM IN THIS COUNTRY! ANY TIME YOU HAVE TOO MANY KIDS LANGUISHING AT OUR BADLY CONGESTED COUNTRY CLUBS, YOU HAVE AN EXPLOSIVE SITUATION!

I THINK EVERY YOUNG MAN OR WOMEN OVER 16 SHOULD BE REQUIRED TO SPEND AT LEAST TWO MONTHS SUMMERING IN EUROPE. I WOULD FAVOR THAT KIND OF PROGRAM.

WHAT IF THEY REFUSED TO GO?

I'D USE FORCE. AFTER CONSULTING WITH THE AFFECTED NATIONS, OF COURSE.

GEORGIA STATE CAPITOL.

YES, MY NAME'S MIKE DOONESBURY, AND I'M WITH THE ANDERSON CAMPAIGN..

I'M CALLING ABOUT THE FILING DEADLINE IN JUNE. IS THE SECRETARY OF STATE IN?

NOPE. GONE FISHIN'!

I SEE. WHAT TIME IS HE EXPECTED BACK?

JULY.

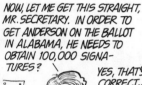

NOW, LET ME GET THIS STRAIGHT, MR. SECRETARY. IN ORDER TO GET ANDERSON ON THE BALLOT IN ALABAMA, HE NEEDS TO OBTAIN 100,000 SIGNATURES?

YES, THAT'S CORRECT..

.. WITH SOME PROVISOS, OF COURSE. THE FIRST 20,000 MUST HAVE MASTER'S DEGREES IN POLITICAL SCIENCE. OF THE REST, 90% MUST BE HOME OWNERS, AND 80% MUST HAVE VOTED IN EVERY ELECTION SINCE 1948.

THAT'S OUTRAGEOUS! THOSE RULES ARE PROHIBITORY AND YOU KNOW IT!

IF YOU DON'T THINK YOU CAN GET THE SIGNATURES, MR. DOONESBURY, WE'D BE HAPPY TO REFUND YOUR APPLICATION FEE.

WE CAN GET 'EM.

YOU CAN? SAY, DID I HAPPEN TO MENTION THE BLOOD TESTS?

BOSS, WE'VE GOT HIS AIDE ON THE LINE. HE SAYS UNFORESEEN CIRCUMSTANCES HAVE KEPT THE OHIO SECRETARY OF STATE FROM PROCESSING OUR BALLOT APPLICATION.

LIKE WHAT?

WHAT UNFORESEEN CIRCUMSTANCES?

HELLO? WHAT UNFORESEEN CIRCUMSTANCES?

HE DIED.

HE DIED.

HE DIED.

DOUBLE-CHECK.

HEY, ZONKER, WHO DO YOU KNOW IN RANCHO MIRAGE, CALIFORNIA?

I GIVE UP, WHO?

BEATS ME. BUT YOU'VE GOT A SPECIAL DELIVERY LETTER.

SPECIAL.. DID YOU SAY RANCHO MIRAGE?

MY GOD! I DON'T BELIEVE IT! I'VE BEEN INVITED TO COMPETE IN THE GERALD R. FORD PRO-AM SUMMER BIATHLON!

CONGRATULATIONS. WHAT'S A SUMMER BIATHLON?

TANNING AND GOLF. THIS IS SUCH AN HONOR!

THE GERALD R. FORD PRO-AM SUMMER BI-ATHLON? WHAT IS A SUMMER BIATHLON, Z.?

IT'S A COMBINA-TION GOLF AND TAN-NING EVENT.

IT'S ONE OF THE MOST PRESTIGIOUS EVENTS OF ITS KIND. USUALLY, ONLY TOP LEISURE SPECIALISTS LIKE BRUCE JENNER ARE INVITED TO PARTICIPATE.

IN PAST YEARS, SOME OF THE TRULY LEGENDARY TANS HAVE BEEN SHOWCASED AT THE FORD BIATHLON — THE '67 SINATRA TAN, THE '73 CHER TAN, THE '77 ANDY WILLIAMS TAN..

YOU MEAN TANNISTS HAVE GOOD AND BAD YEARS?

SURE. EVEN THE BEST. HELL, GEORGE HAMIL-TON'S '63 TAN WAS A **HUGE** SCANDAL.

TELL ME, ZONK, HOW DID OUR FORMER PRESIDENT GET INTERESTED IN THE SUMMER BIATHLON IN THE FIRST PLACE?

WELL, ACCORDING TO THE TOURNAMENT PROGRAM, IT WAS ALL THE RESULT OF A RATHER HAPPY ACCIDENT..

MR. FORD WAS OUT ON THE LINKS ONE DAY WHEN HIS GOLF CART BROKE DOWN. HE DECIDED TO HOOF IT. AT THE END OF THE DAY, HE FOUND THAT NOT ONLY HAD HE SHOT 18 HOLES OF GOLF, BUT HE'D ALSO ACQUIRED A ROSY TAN!

AT THE SAME TIME?

IT WAS SOMETHING OF A BREAK-THROUGH.

I THOUGHT YOU HAD TO TRAIN TODAY, ZONK.

I DO, BUT FIRST I HAVE TO DECIDE WHICH TAN TO GO WITH.

I'VE BEEN GOING THROUGH THE "COPPERTONE GUIDE TO GREAT TANS OF THE SOUTHWEST." SO FAR, I'VE GOT THEM NARROWED DOWN TO "GAUCHO GLOW" AND "ALAMO SUNSET."

"GAUCHO GLOW" IS DESCRIBED AS "ROBUST, FULL-BODIED, A MAN'S TAN, DEEP AND EXCITING." "ALAMO SUNSET" IS "UNPRETENTIOUS BUT TART, AN AMUSING LITTLE COUNTRY TAN."

AN AMUSING LITTLE COUN-TRY TAN?

DON'T LAUGH. IT SWEPT THE GOLD AND SIL-VER AT PHOENIX LAST YEAR.

MIKE, IF ANYONE CALLS, I'LL BE OUT BEHIND THE BARN WORKING ON MY SLICE AND TAN.

OKAY. WHICH TAN DID YOU DECIDE TO SHOOT FOR?

I SETTLED ON A NUMBER CALLED "FREEWAY BOLD." SONNY BONO SPORTED IT DURING HIS UPSET WIN AT THE '79 CHERYL TIEGS DESERT CLASSIC..

THE LITERATURE DESCRIBES IT AS "A FLASHY TROPICAL TAN, A PRE-CANCEROUS GLOW FAVORED BY THE PROS."

SOUNDS PROMISING.

YOU BET IT DOES. TAKE A LOOK AT THESE COL-OR SWATCHES.

HMM.. NOT BAD. BUT DON'T THEY ALWAYS TOUCH THEM UP IN THE BROCHURE?

WELL MET, PILGRIM.

HI, SCOT. WHAT'S SHAKIN'?

BIG NEWS. I'VE JUST RE-CEIVED PERMISSION FROM THE IRANIAN GOVERNMENT TO VISIT THE HOSTAGES.

NO KID-DING? HOW DID YOU SWING THAT?

MY RESUMÉ. APPARENTLY, IT JUST BLEW THEM AWAY—ESPECIALLY MY WORK FOR AMNESTY INTERNATIONAL AND THE ANTI-SHAH DEMONSTRATIONS I USED TO ORGANIZE.

MY ARREST RECORD, OF COURSE, SPOKE FOR ITSELF.

WELL, I KNEW THAT WOULD COME IN HANDY SOONER OR LATER.

SO WHAT EXACTLY ARE YOU PLANNING TO DO IN TEHRAN, SCOT?

WELL, MY MAIN MISSION IS TO VISIT THE HOSTAGES, OF COURSE, TO OFFER THEM COMFORT AND LET THEM KNOW THEY HAVEN'T BEEN FORGOTTEN.

ALSO, IF THE OPPORTUNITY ARISES, I WAS THINKING OF OVERPOWERING ONE OF THE GUARDS AND HOLDING OFF THE OTHERS UNTIL I COULD RADIO FOR ANOTHER RESCUE ATTEMPT.

BUT I DUNNO. PEOPLE MIGHT SEE THAT AS JUST A BIG EGO TRIP.

YEAH. YOU HAVE TO GUARD AGAINST THAT.

SO WHEN DO YOU THINK YOU'LL BE LEAV-ING FOR IRAN, SCOT?

AS SOON AS POSSIBLE, MIKE. I'M TRYING TO GET A FLIGHT OUT TOMORROW.

HAVE YOU RE-CEIVED ALL THE NECESSARY CLEAR-ANCES TO VISIT THE HOSTAGES?

WELL, NOT YET, BUT THEY SHOULD BE FORTH-COMING.

I'VE BEEN ASSURED BY THE IRANIAN GOVERNMENT THAT GETTING PERMISSION FROM THE MILITANTS AND THE REVO-LUTIONARY COUNCIL IS PRETTY MUCH ROUTINE.

YOU BEEN FOLLOWING THIS STORY CLOSELY, REV?

NO, WHY? THEY'RE NOT ABOUT TO RE-LEASE THEM, ARE THEY?

TAXI, SIR?

WHY, YES! CAN YOU TAKE ME INTO TEHRAN?

OF COURSE. WHERE'RE YOU GO-ING, SIR?

ROYAL TEHRAN HILTON.

YOU DO HAVE A WORK ORDER PERSONALLY SIGNED BY THE AYATOLLAH, DON'T YOU, SIR?

A WHAT?

OTHERWISE, I HAVE TO CALL IN THE FARE AND HAVE PARLIAMENT VOTE ON IT.

I REALLY SHOULDN'T BE DRIVING YOU INTO TEHRAN WITHOUT A WORK ORDER FROM THE IMAM. I COULD GET MY HANDS CHOPPED OFF.

WELL, I APPRECIATE YOUR ACCEPTING A BRIBE. I REALLY DO.

IT'S BEEN A WHILE. WE DON'T GET TOO MANY WESTERNERS IN TOWN ANYMORE.

THE ONLY AMERICANS WE'VE SEEN IN MONTHS ARE THE LIARS AND DEMONS OF THE U.S. PRESS. YOU HAIL FROM THE GREAT SATAN YOURSELF, RIGHT?

UH.. RIGHT. NEW YORK, ACTUALLY.

I CAN ALWAYS TELL. HOW LONG YOU BEEN WORKING FOR THE CIA?

ANY SIGN OF THE REV ON THE NEWS, MIKE?

NOT SO FAR.

I GUESS HE HASN'T GOTTEN IN TO SEE THE HOSTAGES YET.

WELL, THAT'S NOT SURPRISING..

HE'S UNDOUBTEDLY GOT A LOT OF HIGH LEVEL NEGOTIATIONS TO GET THROUGH FIRST.

HELLO? OPERATOR? I'M TRYING TO GET ROOM SERVICE.

SORRY, SIR. EVERYONE'S OUT FIGHTING THE LEFTISTS TODAY.

YES?

REVEREND SLOAN, I'M DR. ALI MAHDAVI, I'M FROM THE REVOLUTIONARY COUNCIL.

AT LAST! I WAS BEGINNING TO THINK I'D BEEN FORGOTTEN.

NOT AT ALL. MAY I COME IN?

WHY, OF COURSE, DR. MAHDAVI! PLEASE!

I CAN'T STAY LONG. I LEFT MY MOB OUTSIDE.

DEATH TO CARTER! DEATH TO CARTER!

YOU.. UH..HAVE YOUR OWN MOB?

YES. WE'RE ON OUR WAY TO A FUNERAL.

REVEREND SLOAN, I CAN PERSONALLY ASSURE YOU THAT THE HOSTAGES ARE STILL IN PERFECT PHYSICAL AND MENTAL HEALTH.

BUT AS A MAN OF GOD, YOU SHOULD BE AWARE OF THE STATE OF MORAL TURPITUDE WHICH EXISTS AMONG YOUR COUNTRYMEN..

JUST THIS MORNING, THE STUDENTS CONFISCATED THIS SMUT MAGAZINE FROM ONE OF THE HOSTAGES. LOOK HOW FAR THESE HEATHEN HAVE FALLEN!

GOOD LORD. THESE WOMEN ARE WEARING ..DRESSES!

MANY OF THEM IN BRIGHT COLORS. WE HAVE PROOF THIS MAGAZINE IS PRINTED BY THE CIA.

BUT YOU STILL HAVEN'T SAID WHEN I CAN SEE THE HOSTAGES, DR. MAHDAVI.

ALL IN GOOD TIME, FATHER, ALL IN GOOD TIME.

PERHAPS IF I COULD SPEAK TO SOMEONE IN AUTHORITY..

AUTHORITY? MY DEAR REVEREND, I AM THE AUTHORITY!

THE STUDENTS HAVE BEEN TOLD BY THE IMAM HIMSELF THEY ARE TO ANSWER TO ME! THE WELL-BEING OF THE HOSTAGES IS COMPLETELY IN MY HANDS!

GREAT. ANY IDEA WHERE THEY ARE?

I'M WORKING ON IT. LOOK, WHY DON'T YOU TAKE IN SOME OF THE SIGHTS?

GB Trudeau

HELLO?

REVEREND SLOAN? THIS IS PRESIDENT BANI SADR.

MR. PRESIDENT! BOY, AM I GLAD TO HEAR FROM YOU, SIR. WHEN AM I GOING TO GET TO SEE THE HOSTAGES?

ANY DAY NOW, REVEREND. AS SOON AS WE CAN MAKE ARRANGEMENTS..

I'D RUN YOU OVER TO SEE THEM MYSELF, BUT IT LOOKS LIKE I'M GOING TO BE TIED UP ALL WEEK.

DOING WHAT, SIR?

CLINGING TO POWER. BUT MONDAY FOR SURE, OKAY?

GB Trudeau

STILL NO WORD FROM THE REV. I HOPE HE'S OKAY..

I'M SURE HE'S FINE, MIKE. SAY, YOU GOT THE TIME?

SURE. IT'S ABOUT TEN AFTER ONE.

OH, NO.. I PROMISED MARK I'D CATCH HIS SHOW.

OH? WHO'S HE GOT ON?

FAMED SEXUAL ADVENTURER GAY TALESE. HE'S GOING TO BE READING FROM HIS LATEST MONOGRAPH.

"TALESE SMILED AND REACHED INTO HIS BLACK LEATHERETTE DOCTOR'S BAG.."

DON'T TOUCH THAT DIAL, BOYS AND GIRLS! MORE AFTER THIS..

OVER THE YEARS, WE'VE HAD HIGH PROFILES AND WE'VE HAD LOW PROFILES, BUT FEW SILHOUETTES HAVE LINGERED SO LONG ON THE CULTURAL LANDSCAPE AS THAT OF SEXUAL EXPLORATEUR GAY TALESE.

MR. TALESE IS JUST BACK FROM A NINE-YEAR SAFARI THROUGH THE PORN SHOPS AND MASSAGE PARLORS OF AMERICA, AND HE HAS PUT HIS FINDINGS IN HIS NEW BOOK, "THY NEIGHBOR'S WIFE." MR. TALESE, WHAT'S THE BOOK ABOUT?

WELL, BY WAY OF ANSWERING, IF I MAY, I'D LIKE TO READ SELECTED PASSAGES FROM THE BOOK ITSELF.

WE WERE HOPING YOU'D SAY THAT, MR. TALESE. TAKE IT AWAY.

"IN THE BEGINNING, GAY TALESE DIDN'T EVEN OWN A RAINCOAT.."

YOU'RE KIDDING!

GB Trudeau

"AS TALESE EMERGED FROM HIS '57 TRIUMPH, HIS EYES LOOKED UP HUNGRILY AT THE FLICKERING RED NEON SIGN THAT READ 'LIVE NUDE COEDS'.."

"HE BOUNDED UP THE THREE FLIGHTS OF STEPS, ANXIOUS TO KEEP HIS APPOINTMENT WITH THE VOLUPTUOUS CHEMISTRY MAJOR WHOSE PHOTO HE HAD SELECTED WITH SUCH CARE FROM THE MASSAGE PARLOR PICTURE BOOK."

"WHEN THEY WERE FINALLY ALONE TALESE TURNED TO HER AND SAID, 'I WANT TO JOIN YOUR SILENT REVOLUTION OF THE SENSES, YOUR DEPARTURE FROM CONVENTIONALITY.' THE MASSEUSE SMILED AND REACHED FOR THE POWDER."

"MEANWHILE, OUT IN THE CAR, TALESE'S WIFE WAS GROWING IMPATIENT.."

UNDER-STANDABLY!

"IT WAS CLEAR TO TALESE THAT THE MASSAGE PARLOR WAS ON THE CUTTING EDGE OF THE NEW REVOLUTION.."

BUT YOU STILL HAVEN'T TOLD US WHAT THE BOOK'S ABOUT, MR. TALESE..

I'M GETTING TO THAT. "AS THE WEEKS PASSED, TALESE GREW CURIOUS ABOUT HIS FELLOW MASSAGE PARLOR PATRONS. HE DECIDED TO GIVE THEM THE OPPORTUNITY TO CONFIDE IN HIM."

"AFTER MONTHS OF SKILLFUL AND SENSITIVE INTERVIEWS, ONE OF THE CUSTOMERS FINALLY REVEALED THAT HE WAS MIDDLE-CLASS AND MARRIED. DAYS LATER, ANOTHER JOHN CONFESSED THAT HE, TOO, WAS MIDDLE-CLASS AND MARRIED."

"TALESE KNEW A TREND WHEN HE SAW ONE."

WOW.. I GUESS THAT'S THE ADVANTAGE OF BEING A REPORTER.

"NOTHING TALESE HAD EVER SEEN PREPARED HIM FOR THE EXPERIMENTS IN OPEN SEXUALITY HE WAS TO WITNESS THAT NIGHT AT THE SANDSTONE RETREAT.."

"ONLY A FEW FEET AWAY, SEXUAL PIONEERS WERE BREAKING NEW GROUND, PUSHING THE BOUNDARIES OF HONEST, OPEN COMMUNICATION BEYOND THE OUTER REACHES OF ACCEPTED SOCIAL BEHAVIOR."

"TALESE WENT UPSTAIRS WITH THREE OF HIS FELLOW REVOLUTIONARIES, AND FOR THE NEXT SEVERAL HOURS FLOUTED CONVENTION. SO PREOCCUPIED DID HE BECOME WITH HIS SILENT PROTEST AGAINST THE CENSORS AND CLERICS, HE FAILED TO HEAR A KNOCK."

"TALESE LOOKED UP TO SEE FOUR MORE PIONEERS."

HARDY STOCK, I HOPE.

HELLO?

REVEREND SLOAN? IT'S PRESIDENT BANI SADR.

YES, MR. PRESIDENT.

WE HAVE LOCATED THE HOSTAGES. DR. MAHDAVI WILL BE BY SHORTLY TO TAKE YOU TO THEM.

HELLO, REVEREND? DON'T LISTEN TO HIM! HE CAN'T DELIVER!

HEY! WHO'S THAT? IS THAT YOU, BEHESHTI?

HE DOESN'T HAVE THE AYATOLLAH'S EAR!

I DO, TOO! GET OFF THE LINE, YOU INSECT!